Why Businessmen Need Philosophy

by

Ayn Rand

with additional articles by

Leonard Peikoff

Harry Binswanger, Edwin A. Locke,
John B. Ridpath, Richard M. Salsman and
Jaana Woiceshyn

edited by

Richard E. Ralston

First Printing January 1999
10 9 8 7 6 5 4 3 2 1

http://www.aynrand.org/

ISBN: 0-9625336-2-9

Manufactured in the United States of America

Production by Ronen Nakash
Cover design by Klaus Nordby

Table of Contents

Introduction

*Ideas are the greatest and
most crucially practical
power on earth.*
                —Ayn Rand

The idea for this project originated with Ayn Rand's heir, Leonard Peikoff, who prepared the title essay as a talk to the New York chapter of the Young Presidents' Organization on January 12, 1995. The viewpoint of this and the other essays is that businessmen do need philosophy. Philosophy is not an ivory tower escape from the real world but a practical necessity involved in every aspect of the real world, from everyday business dealings to the broadest issues of politics and economics. Without the right philosophy as a basis and defense, the free marketplace of goods and ideas will disappear.

These essays—including two by Ayn Rand published in book form for the first time—illustrate the importance of philosophy to business in general and to such related topics as antitrust, the environment, free trade, racism in the workplace and business ethics.

Why Businessmen Need Philosophy is published in tribute to businessmen everywhere who understand the need proudly to defend the moral stature of their profession.

Richard E. Ralston
Editor

Why Businessmen
Need Philosophy

Leonard Peikoff

"Three seconds remain, the ball is on the one-yard line, here it is—the final play—a touchdown for Dallas! The Cowboys defeat the Jets 24–23!" The crowd roars, the cheering swells. Suddenly, silence.

Everyone remembers that today is the start of a new policy: morality in sports. The policy was conceived at Harvard, championed by the *New York Times,* and enacted into law by a bipartisan majority in Washington.

The announcer's voice booms out again: "Today's game is a big win for New York! Yes, you heard me. It's wrong for athletes to be obsessed with competition, money, personal gratification. No more dog-eat-dog on the field, no more materialism— no more selfishness! The new law of the game is self-sacrifice: place the other team above yourself, it is better to give than to receive! Dallas therefore loses. As a condition of playing today it had to agree to surrender its victory to the Jets. As we all know, the Jets need a victory badly, and so do their fans. Need is what counts now. Need, not quarterbacking skill; weakness, not strength; help to the unfortunate, not rewards to the already powerful."

Nobody boos—it certainly sounds like what you hear in church—but nobody cheers, either. "Football will never be the same," mutters a man to his son. The two look down at the ground and shrug. "What's wrong with the world?" the boy asks.

The basic idea of this fantasy, the idea that self-sacrifice is the essence of virtue, is no fantasy. It is all around us, though not yet in football. Nobody defends selfishness any more: not conservatives, not liberals; not religious people, not atheists; not Republicans, not Democrats.

White males, for instance, should not be so "greedy," we hear regularly; they should sacrifice more for women and the minorities. Both employers and employees are callous, we hear; they spend their energy worrying about their own futures, trying to become even richer, when they should be concerned with serving their customers. Americans are far too affluent, we hear; they should be transferring some of their abundance to the poor, both at home and abroad.

If a poor man finds a job and rises to the level of buying his own health insurance, for instance, that is not a moral achievement, we are told; he is being selfish, merely looking out for his own or his family's welfare. But if the same man receives his health care free from Washington, using a credit card or a law made by Bill Clinton, that is idealistic and noble. Why? Because sacrifice is involved: sacrifice extorted from employers, by the employers' mandate, and from doctors through a noose of new regulations around their necks.

If America fights a war in which we have a national interest, such as oil in the Persian Gulf, we hear that the war is wrong because it is selfish. But if we invade some foreign pesthole for no selfish reason, with no national interest involved, as in Bosnia, Somalia or Haiti, we hear praise from the intellectuals. Why? Because we are being selfless.

The Declaration of Independence states that all men have an inalienable right to "life, liberty, and the pursuit of happiness." What does the "pursuit of happiness" mean? Jefferson does not say that you have a duty to pursue your neighbor's pleasure or the collective American well-being, let alone the aspirations of the Bosnians. He upholds a selfish principle: each man has the right to live for his own sake, his own personal interests, his own happiness. He does not say: run roughshod over others, or: violate their rights. But he does say: pursue your own goals independently, by your own work, and respect every other individual's right to do the same for himself.

In essence, America was conceived by egoists. The Founding Fathers envisioned a land of selfishness and profit-seeking— a nation of the self-made man, the individual, the ego, the "I." Today, however, we hear the opposite ideas everywhere.

Who are the greatest victims of today's attitude? Who are the most denounced and vilified men in the country? *You* are— you, the businessmen. And the bigger and better you are, the worse you are morally, according to today's consensus. You are denounced for one sin: you are the epitome of selfishness.

In fact, you really are selfish. You are selfish in the noblest sense, which is inherent in the very nature of business: you seek to make a profit, the greatest profit possible—by selling at the highest price the market will bear while buying at the lowest price. You seek to make money—gigantic amounts of it, the more the better—in small part to spend on personal luxury, but largely to put back into your business, so that it will grow still further and make even greater profits.

As a businessman, you make your profit by being the best you can be in your work, i.e., by creating goods or services that your customers want. You profit not by fraud or robbery, but by producing wealth and trading with others. You do benefit other people, or the so-called "community," but this is a secondary consequence of your action. It is not and cannot be your primary focus or motive.

The great businessman is like a great musician, or a great man in any field. The composer focuses on creating his music; his goal is to express his ideas in musical form, the particular form which most gratifies and fulfills him himself. If the audience enjoys his concerto, of course he is happy—there is no clash between him and his listeners—but his listeners are not his primary concern. His life is the exercise of his creative power to achieve his own selfish satisfaction. He could not function or compose otherwise. If he were not moved by a powerful, personal, selfish passion, he could not wring out of himself the necessary energy, effort, time and labor; he could not endure the daily frustrations of the creative process. This is true of every creative man. It is also true of you in business, to the extent that you are great, i.e., to the extent that you are creative in organization, management, long-range planning, and their result: production.

Business to a creative man *is* his life. His life is not the social results of the work, but the work itself, the actual job—the thought, the blueprints, the decisions, the deals, the action. Creativity is inherently selfish; productivity is inherently selfish.

The opposite of selfishness is altruism. Altruism does not mean kindness to others, nor respect for their rights, both of which are perfectly possible to selfish men, and indeed widespread among them. Altruism is a term coined by the nineteenth-century French philosopher, Auguste Comte, who based it on the Latin "alter," meaning "other." Literally, the term means: "otherism." By Comte's definition and ever since, it means: "placing others above oneself as the basic rule of life." This means not helping another out occasionally, if he deserves it and you can afford it, but *living* for others unconditionally—living and, above all, sacrificing for them; sacrificing your own interests, your own pleasures, your own values.

What would happen to a business if it were actually run by an altruist? Such a person knows nothing about creativity or its requirements. What *his* creed tells him is only: "Give up. Give up and give away; give away to and for others." What should he give away? Whatever is there; whatever he has access to; whatever somebody else has created.

Either a man cares about the process of production, or he does not. If he cares about the process, it must be his primary concern; not the beneficiaries of the process, but the personal fulfillment inherent in his own productive activity. If he does not care about it, then he cannot produce.

If the welfare of others were your primary aim, then you would have to dismantle your business. For instance, you would have to hire needy workers, regardless of their competence— whether or not they lead you to a profit. Why do you care about profit, anyway? As an altruist, you seek to sacrifice yourself and your business, and these workers need the jobs. Further, why charge customers the highest price you can get—isn't that selfish? What if your customers need the product desperately? Why not simply give away goods and services as they are needed? An altruist running a business like a social work project would be a destroyer—but not for long, since he would soon go broke. Do you see Albert Schweitzer running General Motors? Would you have prospered with Mother Teresa as the CEO of your company?

Many businessmen recognize that they are selfish, but feel guilty about it and try to appease their critics. These businessmen, in their speeches and advertisements, regularly proclaim that they are really selfless, that their only concern is the welfare of their workers, their customers, and their stockholders, especially the widows and orphans among them. Their own profit, they say, is really not very big, and next year, they promise, they will give even more of it away. No one believes any of this, and these businessmen look like nothing but what they are: hypocrites. One way or another, everyone knows that these men are denying the essence and purpose of their work. This kind of PR destroys any positive image of business in the public mind. If you yourselves, by your own appeasement, damn your real motives and activity, why should anyone else evaluate you differently?

Some of you may reply: "But I really am an altruist. I do live for a higher purpose. I don't care excessively about myself or even my family. I really want primarily to serve the needy." This is a possible human motive—it is a shameful motive, but a possible one. If it *is* your motive, however, you will not be a successful businessman, not for long. Why is it shameful? Let me answer by asking the altruists among you: Why do you have such low self-esteem? Why don't you and those you love deserve to be the beneficiaries of *your* efforts. Are you excluded from the Declaration of Independence merely because you are a businessman? Does a producer have no right to happiness? Does success turn you into a slave?

You do not expect your workers to say, "We don't care about ourselves; we're only servants of the public and of our bosses." In fact, labor says the exact opposite. Your workers stand up proudly and say, "We work hard for a living. We deserve a reward, and we damn well expect to get it!" Observe that the country respects such workers and their attitude. Why then are businessmen supposed to be serfs? Aren't you as good as the rest of mankind? Why should you alone spend your precious time sweating selflessly for a reward that is to be given to someone else?

The best among you do not believe the altruist mumbo-jumbo. You have, however, long been disarmed by it. Because you are the victim of a crucial power, against which you are helpless. That power is philosophy.

This brings us to the question of why businessmen need philosophy.

The issue with which we began—selfishness vs. altruism—is a philosophic issue; specifically, it is a moral or ethical issue. One of the important questions of ethics is: should a man live for himself, or should he sacrifice for something beyond himself? In the medieval era, for example, philosophers held that selfishness was wicked, that men must sacrifice themselves for God. In such an era, there was no possibility of an institutionalized system of profit-seeking companies. To the medievals, business would represent sheer wickedness.

This philosophy gradually changed, across centuries, culminating in the view of Jefferson, who championed the selfish pursuit of one's own happiness. He took this idea from John Locke, who got it, ultimately, from Aristotle, the real father of selfishness in ethics. Jefferson's defense of the right to happiness made possible the founding of America and of a capitalist system. Since the eighteenth century, however, the philosophic pendulum has swung all the way back to the medieval period. Today, once again, self-sacrifice is extolled as the moral ideal.

Why should you care about this philosophic history? As a practical man, you must care; because it is an issue of life and death. It is a simple syllogism. Premise one: Businessmen are selfish; which everyone knows, whatever denials or protestations they hear. Premise two: Selfishness is wicked; which almost everyone today, including the appeasers among you, thinks is self-evident. The inescapable conclusion: Businessmen are wicked. If so, you are the perfect scapegoats for intellectuals of every kind to blame for every evil or injustice that occurs, whether real or trumped up.

If you think that this is merely theory, look at reality—at today's culture—and observe what the country thinks of business these days. Popular movies provide a good indication. Do not bother with such obviously left-wing movies as *Wall Street,* the product of avowed radicals and business-haters. Consider rather the highly popular Tim Allen movie, *The Santa Clause.* It was a simple children's fantasy about Santa delivering gifts; it was seasonal family trivia that upheld no abstract ideas or philosophy, the kind of movie which expressed only safe, non-controversial, self-evident sentiments. In the middle of the movie, with no plot purpose of any kind, the story leaves Santa to show two "real businessmen": toy manufacturers scheming gleefully to swindle the country's children with inferior products (allegedly, to make greater profits thereby). After which, the characters vanish, never to be seen again. It was a sheer throwaway—and the audience snickers along with it approvingly, as though there is no controversy here. "Everybody knows that's the way businessmen are."

Imagine the national outcry if any other minority—and you are a very small minority—were treated like this. If a "quickie" scene were inserted into a movie to show that females are swindlers, or gays, or blacks—the movie would be denounced, reedited, sanitized, apologized for and pulled from the theaters. But businessmen? Money-makers and profit-seekers? In regard to them, anything goes, because they are wicked, i.e., selfish. They are "pigs," "robbers," "villains"—everyone knows that! Incidentally, to my knowledge, not one businessman or group of them protested against this movie.

There are hundreds of such movies, and many more books, TV shows, sermons and college lectures, all expressing the same ideas. Are such ideas merely talk, with no practical consequences for you and your balance sheets? The principal consequence is this: once you are deprived of moral standing, you are fair game.

No matter what you do or how properly you act, you will be accused of the most outrageous evils. Whether the charges are true or false is irrelevant. If you are fundamentally evil, as the public has been taught to think, then any accusation against you is plausible—you are, people think, capable of anything.

If so, the politicians can then step in. They can blame you for anything, and pass laws to hogtie and expropriate you. After all, everyone feels, you must have obtained your money dishonestly; you are in business! The anti-trust laws are an eloquent illustration of this process at work. If some official in Washington decides that your prices are "too high," for instance, it must be due to your being a "monopolist": your business, therefore, must be broken up, and you should be fined or jailed. Or, if the official feels that your prices are "too low," you are probably an example of "cutthroat competition," and deserve to be punished. Or, if you try to avoid both these paths by setting a common price with your competitors—neither too high or too low, but just right—*that* is "conspiracy." Whatever you do, you are guilty.

Whatever happens anywhere today is your fault and guilt. Some critics point to the homeless and blame their poverty on greedy private businessmen who exploit the public. Others, such as John Kenneth Galbraith, say that Americans are too affluent and too materialistic, and blame greedy private businessmen, who corrupt the masses by showering them with ads and goods. Ecologists claim that our resources are vanishing and blame it on businessmen, who squander natural resources for selfish profit. If a broker dares to take any financial advantage from a lifetime of study and contacts in his field, he is guilty of "insider trading." If racial discrimination is a problem, businessmen must pay for it by hiring minority workers, whether qualified or not. If sexual harassment is a problem, businessmen are the villains; they must be fondling their downtrodden filing clerks, as they leave for the bank to swindle the poor widows and orphans. The litany is unmistakable: if anybody has any trouble of any kind, blame the businessman—even if a customer spills a cup of her coffee miles away from the seller's establishment. By definition, business-men have unlimited liability. They are guilty of every conceiv-able crime because they are guilty of the worst, lowest crime: selfishness.

The result is an endless stream of political repercussions: more laws, more controls, more regulations, more alleged crimes, more fines, more lawsuits, more bureaus, more taxes, more need to bow down on your knees before Washington, Albany or Giuliani, begging for favors, merely to survive. All of this means: the methodical and progressive enslavement of business.

No other group in the world would stand for or put up with such injustice—not plumbers or philosophers, not even Bosnians or Chechens. Any other group, in outrage, would assert its rights—real or alleged—and demand justice. Businessmen, however, do not. They are disarmed because they know that the charge of selfishness is true.

Instead of taking pride in your selfish motives and fighting back, you are ashamed, undercut and silent. This is what philoso-phy—bad philosophy—and specifically a bad code of morality has done to you. Just as such a code would destroy football, so now it is destroying the United States.

Today, there is a vicious double-standard in the American justice system. Compare the treatment of accused criminals with that of accused businessmen. For example: if a man (like O.J. Simpson) commits a heinous double-murder, mobs everywhere chant that he is innocent until proven guilty. Millions rush to his defense, he buys half the legal profession and is acquitted of his crimes. Whereas, if a businessman invents a brilliant method of financing business ventures through so-called junk bonds, thereby becoming a meteoric success while violating not one man's rights, he is guilty—guilty by definition, guilty of being a businessman—

and he must pay multi-million-dollar fines, perform years of community service, stop working in his chosen profession, and even spend many years in jail.

If, in the course of pursuing your selfish profits, you really did injure the public, then the attacks on you would have some justification. But the opposite is true. You make your profits by production and you trade freely with your customers, thereby showering wealth and benefits on everyone. (I refer here to businessmen who stand on their own and actually produce in a free market, not those who feed at the public trough for subsidies, bailouts, tariffs and government-dispensed monopolies.)

Now consider the essential nature of running a business and the qualities of character it requires.

There is an important division of labor not taught in our colleges. Scientists discover the laws of nature. Engineers and inventors apply those laws to develop ideas for new products. Laborers will work to produce these goods if they are given a salary and a prescribed task, i.e., a plan of action and a productive purpose to guide their work. These people and professions are crucial to an economy. But they are not enough. If all we had was scientific knowledge, untried ideas for new products, and directionless physical labor, we would starve.

The indispensable element here—the crucial "spark plug," which ignites the best of every other group, transforming merely potential wealth into the abundance of a modern industrial society—is business.

Businessmen accumulate capital through production and savings. They decide in which future products to invest their savings. They have the crucial task of integrating natural resources, human discoveries and physical labor. They must organize, finance and manage the productive process, or choose, train and oversee the men competent to do it. These are the demanding, risk-laden decisions and actions on which abundance and prosperity depend. Profit represents success in regard to these decisions and actions. Loss represents failure. Philosophically, therefore, profit is a payment earned by moral virtue—by the highest moral virtue. It is payment for the thought, the initiative, the long-range vision, the courage and the efficacy of the economy's prime movers: the businessmen.

Your virtue confers blessings on every part of society. By creating mass markets, you make new products available to every income level. By organizing productive enterprises, you create employment for men in countless fields. By using machines, you increase the productivity of labor, thus raising the working-man's pay and rewards. The businessman, to quote Ayn Rand,

> is the great liberator who, in the short span of a century and a half, has released men from bondage to their physical needs, has released them from the terrible drudgery of an eighteen-hour workday of manual labor for their barest subsistence, has released them from famines, from pestilences, from the stagnant hopelessness and terror in which most of mankind had lived in all the pre-capitalist centuries—and in which most of it still lives, in non-capitalist countries.[1]

If businessmen are such great liberators, you can be sure that those who denounce you know this fact. The truth is that you are denounced partly because you *are* mankind's great providers and liberators, which raises another critical topic.

Selfishness is not the only virtue for which you are damned by today's intellectuals. They invoke two other philosophical issues as a club to condemn you with: reality and reason.

By "reality," I mean the universe around us; the material world in which we live and which we observe with our senses: the earth, the planets, the galaxies. As businessmen you are committed to this world, not to any other dimension alleged to transcend it. You are not in business to secure or offer supernatural rewards, other-worldly bliss or the welfare of an ecological rose

---

[1] Rand, A. *For the New Intellectual.* New York: New American Library, 1961, p. 27.

garden in the twenty-fifth century. You pursue real, this-worldly values, here and now. You produce physical goods and tangible services. You seek monetary profit, which you intend to invest or spend now. You do not offer your customers out-of-body experiences, UFO rides or reincarnation as Shirley MacLaine. You offer real, earthly pleasures; you make possible physical products, rational services and the actual enjoyment of this life.

This completely contradicts many major philosophical schools. It puts you into conflict with every type of supernaturalist, from the medieval-style theists on through today's "New Age" spiritualists and mystics. All these people like to demean this life and this world in favor of another, undefined existence in the beyond: to be found in heaven, in nirvana or on LSD. Whatever they call it, this other realm is beyond the reach of science and logic.

If these supernaturalists are right, then your priorities as businessmen—your philosophic priorities—are dead wrong. If the material world is, as they claim, "low, vulgar, crude, unreal," then so are you who cater to it. You are materialistic animals devoted to inferior physical concerns. By showering men with material values, you are corrupting and debasing them, as Galbraith says, rather than truly liberating them.

A businessman *must* be worldly and concerned with the physical. From the physical laws ruling your assembly line, to the cold, hard facts of your financial accounts, business is a materialistic enterprise. This is another reason why there could be no such thing as business in the medieval era: not only selfishness, but *worldliness*, was considered a major sin. This same combination of charges—selfishness and materialism—is unleashed against you today by the modern equivalent of the medieval mentality. The conclusion they reach is the same: "Down with business!"

The third philosophic issue is the validity of reason. Reason is the human faculty which forms concepts by a process of logic based on the evidence of the senses; reason is our means of gaining knowledge of this world and guiding our actions in it. By the nature of their field, businessmen must be committed to reason, at least in their professional lives. You do not make business decisions by consulting tea leaves, the "Psychic Friends Network," the Book of Genesis, or any other kind of mystic revelation. If you tried to do it, then like all gamblers who bet on blind intuition, you would be ruined.

Successful businessmen have to be men of the intellect. Many people believe that wealth is a product of purely physical factors, such as natural resources and physical labor. But both of these have been abundant throughout history and are in poverty-stricken nations still today, such as India, Russia and throughout Africa.

Wealth is primarily a product not of physical factors, but of the human mind—of the intellectual faculty—of the rational, thinking faculty. I mean here the mind not only of scientists and engineers, but also the mind of those men and women—the businessmen—who organize knowledge and resources into industrial enterprises.

Primarily, it is the reason and intelligence of great industrialists that make possible electric generators, computers, coronary-bypass surgical instruments and spaceships.

If you are to succeed in business, you must make decisions using logic. You must deal with objective realities—like them or not. Your life is filled with numbers, balance sheets, cold efficiency and rational organization. You have to make sense—to your employees, to your customers, and to yourself. You cannot run a business as a gambler plays the horses, or as a cipher wailing, "Who am I to know? My mind is helpless. I need a message from God, Nancy Reagan's astrologer or Eleanor Roosevelt's soul." You have to *think*.

The advocates of a supernatural realm never try to prove its existence by reason. They claim that they have a means of knowledge superior to reason, such as intuition, hunch, faith, subjective feeling or the "seat of their pants." Reason is their enemy, because it is the tool that will expose their racket: so they condemn it and its advocates as cold, analytic, unfeeling, straight-jacketed, narrow, limited. By their standard, anyone devoted to reason and logic is a low mentality, fit only to be ruled by those with superior mystic insight. This argument originated with Plato in the ancient world, and it is still going strong today. It is another crucial element in the anti-business philosophy.

To summarize, there are three fundamental questions central to any philosophy, which every person has to answer in some way: What is there? How do you know it? And, what should you do?

The Founding Fathers had answers to these questions. What is there? "This world," they answered, "nature." (Although they believed in God, it was a pale deist shadow of the medieval period. For the Founding Fathers, God was a mere bystander, who had set the world in motion but no longer interfered.) How did they know? Reason was "the only oracle of man," they said. What should you do? "Pursue your own happiness," said Jefferson. The result of these answers—i.e., of their total philosophy—was capitalism, freedom and individual rights. This brought about a century of international peace, and the rise of the business mentality, leading to the magnificent growth of industry and of prosperity.

For two centuries since, the enemies of the Founding Fathers have given the exact opposite answers to these three questions. What is there? "Another reality," they say. How do they know? "On faith." What should you do? "Sacrifice yourself for society." This is the basic philosophy of our culture, and it is responsible for the accelerating collapse of capitalism, and all of its symptoms: runaway government trampling on individual rights, growing economic dislocations, worldwide tribal warfare and international terrorism—with business under constant, systematic attack.

Such is the philosophic choice you have to make. Such are the issues on which you will ultimately succeed or fail. If the anti-business philosophy with its three central ideas continues to dominate this country and to spread, then businessmen as such will become extinct, as they were in the Middle Ages and in Soviet Russia. They will be replaced by church authorities or government commissars. Your only hope for survival is to fight this philosophy by embracing a rational, worldly, selfish alternative.

We are all trained by today's colleges never to take a firm stand on any subject: to be pragmatists, ready to compromise with anyone on anything. Philosophy and morality, however, do not work by compromise. Just as a healthy body cannot compromise with poison, so too a good man cannot compromise with evil ideas. In such a set up, an evil philosophy, like poison, always wins. The good can win only by being consistent. If it is not, then the evil is given the means to win every time.

For example, if a burglar breaks into your house and demands your silverware, you have two possible courses of action. You might take a militant attitude: shoot him or at least call the police. That is certainly uncompromising. You have taken the view, "What's mine is mine, and there is no bargaining about it." Or, you might "negotiate" with him, try to be conciliatory, and persuade him to take only half your silverware. Whereupon you relax, pleased with your seemingly successful compromise, until he returns next week demanding the rest of your silverware— and your money, your car and your wife. Because you have agreed that his arbitrary, unjust demand gives him a right to *some* of your property, the only negotiable question thereafter is: how much? Sooner or later he will take everything. You compromised; he won.

The same principle applies if the government seeks to expropriate you or regulate your property. If the government floats a trial balloon to the effect that it will confiscate or control all industrial property over $10 million in the name of the public good, you have two possible methods of fighting back. You might stand on principle—in this case, the principle of private property and individual rights—and refuse to compromise, you might resolve to fight to the end for your rights and actually do so in your advertisements, speeches and press releases. Given the better elements in the American people, it is possible for you by this means to win substantial support and defeat such a measure. The alternative course, and the one that business has unfortunately taken throughout the decades, is to compromise—for example, by making a deal conceding that the government can take over in New Jersey, but not in New York. This amounts to saying: "Washington, D.C., has no right to all our property, only some of it." As with the burglar, the government will soon take over everything. You have lost all you have as soon as you say the fatal words, "I compromise."

I do not advise you to break any law, but I do advise you to fight an *intellectual* battle against big government, as many medical doctors did, with real success, against Clinton's health plan. You may be surprised at how much a good philosophical fight will accomplish for your public image, and also for your pocketbook. For instance, an open public fight for a flat tax, for the end of the capital gains and estate taxes, and for the privatizing of welfare and the gradual phasing out of all government entitlements is urgent. More important than standing for these policies, however, is doing so righteously, not guiltily and timidly. If you understand the philosophic issues involved, you will have a chance to speak up in such a way that you can be heard.

This kind of fight is not easy, but it can be fought and won. Years ago, a well-known political writer, Isabel Paterson, was talking to a businessman outraged by some government action. She urged him to speak up for his principles. "I agree with you totally," he said, "but I'm not in a position right now to do it."

"The only position required," she replied, "is vertical."

The Money-Making Personality

Ayn Rand

Ayn Rand's tribute to "the money-making personality" was first published in Cosmopolitan *in April 1963.*

The Money-Making Personality

Ayn Rand

Suppose that you have observed two young men on their way through college and, on graduation day, are asked to tell which one of them will make a fortune.

Let us call them Smith and Jones. Both are intelligent, ambitious and come from the same modestly average background. But there are significant differences between them.

Smith is aggressively social and very popular; he belongs to many campus groups and is usually their leader. Jones is quiet, reserved; he does not join group activities; he is usually noticed, but neither liked nor disliked; some people resent him for no apparent reason.

Smith has a wide variety of interests, but is always available for one more undertaking. Jones has chosen an undertaking—the pursuit of some special task or study outside the college curriculum—to which he devotes all of his spare time.

Smith adjusts himself to people easily, but finds it harder to adjust himself to changing circumstances. Jones adjusts himself to circumstances, but is inflexible in regard to people.

Smith's scholastic grades are uniformly excellent. Jones's grades are irregular: he rates "A plus" in some subjects and "C" in others.

Smith's image in people's minds is one of sunny cheerfulness. Jones's image is grimly earnest. But some rare, fleeting signs seem to indicate that in the privacy of their inner worlds their roles are reversed: it is Jones who is serenely cheerful, and Smith who is driven by some grimly nameless dread.

Which one would you choose as the future fortune-maker?

If you subscribe to the currently prevalent ideas, you would choose Smith—and you would be wrong. Jones is the archetype of the Money-Maker, while Smith is a deceptive facsimile who will never *make* money, though he may become rich; to describe him accurately, one would have to call him the "Money-Appropriator."

Prospectors looking for gold know that there exists a mineral which deceives the ignorant by its brilliant glitter: they call it fool's gold. A similar distinction exists between the real producers of wealth and the pseudo-producers, but the mineralogists of the human soul have not learned to differentiate between them.

Most people lump together into the same category all men who become rich, refusing to consider the essential question: the *source* of the riches, the means by which the wealth was acquired.

Money is a tool of exchange; it represents wealth only so long as it can be traded for material goods and services. Wealth does not grow in nature; it has to be produced by men. Nature gives us only the raw materials, but it is man's mind that has to discover the knowledge of how to use them. It is man's thinking and labor that transform the materials into food, clothing, shelter or television sets—into all the goods that men require for their survival, comfort and pleasure.

Behind every step of humanity's long climb from the cave to New York City, there is the man who took that step for the first time—the man who discovered how to make a fire or a wheel or an airplane or an electric light.

When people refuse to consider the source of wealth, what they refuse to recognize is the fact that *wealth is the product of man's intellect,* of his creative ability, fully as much as is art, science, philosophy or any other human value.

The Money-*Maker* is the discoverer who translates his discovery into material goods. In an industrial society with a complex division of labor, it may be one man or a partnership of two: the scientist who discovers new knowledge and the *entrepreneur*—the businessman—who discovers how to use that knowledge, how to organize material resources and human labor into an enterprise producing marketable goods.

The Money-*Appropriator* is an entirely different type of man. He is essentially noncreative—and his basic goal is to acquire an unearned share of the wealth created by others. He seeks to get rich, not by conquering nature, but by manipulating men, not by intellectual effort, but by social maneuvering. He does not produce, he redistributes: he merely switches the wealth already in existence from the pockets of its owners to his own.

The Money-Appropriator may become a politician—or a businessman who "cuts corners"—or that destructive product of a "mixed economy": the businessman who grows rich by means of government favors, such as special privileges, subsidies, franchises; that is, grows rich by means of *legalized force*.

In the present state of our economy, in the chaotic mixture of free enterprise and government controls, it is becoming progressively harder to distinguish the Money-Maker from the Money-Appropriator. When every business is tangled in government regulations, the dividing line between the earned and the unearned grows blurred. Authentic Money-Makers are forced to resort to government help—and some Money-Appropriators are forced, at times, to exercise some productive effort, if only for the sake of their "public image." But if one watches a man's activity over a period of time, one can still see whether his success is due essentially to his productive ability or to political pull.

No single outward characteristic can be taken as a sure sign of the Money-Making personality. The traits ascribed to Smith and Jones may vary. But the net sum of their traits will always add up to the same essentials: the essential characteristic of the Money-Maker is his *independent judgment;* the essential characteristic of the Money-Appropriator is his *social dependence.*

A man of independent judgment is a man of profound self-esteem: he trusts the competence of his own mind to deal with the problems of existence. He looks at the world, wondering: "What can be done?" or "How can things be improved?"

The Money-Maker, above all else, is the originator and innovator. The trait most signally absent from his character is *resignation,* the passive acceptance of the given, the known, the established, the *status quo.* He never says: "What was good enough for my grandfather is good enough for me." He says: "What was good enough for me yesterday will not be good enough tomorrow."

He does not sit waiting for "a break" or for somebody to give him a chance. He makes and takes his own chances. He never whines, "I couldn't help it!"—he *can,* and does.

The men who will never make money are: the hedger who "plays it safe," waiting to follow any trend, and the gambler or plunger who plays blind hunches, on the spur of the moment, on hearsay, on his own unaccountable feelings.

The Money-Maker does neither. He does not wait for trends—he sets them. He does not gamble—he takes calculated risks, assuming the very responsibility which those two attempt to bypass: the responsibility of judgment.

The man who will never make money has an "employee mentality," even in an executive's job; he tries to get away with a minimum of effort, as if any exertion were an imposition; and when he fails to take the proper action, he cries: "But nobody told me to!"

The Money-Maker has an "employer mentality," even when he is only an office boy—which is why he does not remain an office boy for long. In any job he holds, he is committed to a maximum of effort; he learns evervthing he can about the business, much more than his job requires. He never needs to be told— even when confronting a situation outside his usual duties. These are the reasons why he rises from office boy to company president.

Behind his usually grim, expressionless face, the Money-Maker is committed to his work with the passion of a lover, the fire of a crusader, the dedication of a saint and the endurance of a martyr. As a rule, his creased forehead and his balance sheets are the only evidence of it he can allow the world to see.

Neither space, time nor age can limit the Money-Maker's extravagant energy and drive.

At the age of twenty-two, George Westinghouse observed the frequency of railroad accidents caused by inadequate brakes— and invented the Westinghouse Air Brake which, with some improvements, is used to this day on all trains throughout the world.

At the age of sixty-nine, Cornelius Vanderbilt—who had made a fortune in the shipping business—saw that railroads were to be the chief transportation medium of the future, gave up shipping and became one of the greatest figures in our railroad history, the creator of the New York Central system.

Arthur Vining Davis, who died in 1962 at the age of ninety-five, was the man who built, singlehanded, one of America's greatest industrial concerns: Alcoa (Aluminum Company of America). He joined it at the age of twenty-one, "almost literally as the first hired hand," wrote *Fortune*. "In the decades following the turn of the century, when Alcoa *was* the aluminum industry, A. V. Davis *was* Alcoa." His associates said that he had "absolute confidence in his own business acumen and judgment." He was described as follows: "He has a fierce impatience to get things done . . . is intolerably intolerant of wits less nimble than his own . . . and has a noble temper."

At the age of eighty-nine, with a fortune estimated at $350,000,000, Davis moved to Florida and embarked upon an entirely new career that involved a fantastic variety of new interests: Florida real estate developments, nurseries, airlines, hotels, banks, dairy farms, etc.—all of which he proceeded to manage with splendid efficiency and growing success. When he was questioned about his goals, he answered brusquely, "I buy properties with the thought of making money."

Observe that his new ventures were long-range developments which required decades before they could pay off. The men who dream of winning a fortune on a sweepstakes ticket would never understand his psychology.

It is only the Money-Appropriator who lives and acts short-range, never looking beyond the immediate moment. The Money-Maker lives, thinks and acts long-range. Having complete confidence in his own judgment, he has complete confidence in the future, and only long-range projects can hold his interest. To a Money-Maker, as well as to an artist, work is not a painful duty or a necessary evil, but *a way of life;* to him, productive activity is the essence, the meaning and the enjoyment of existence; it is the state of being alive.

Arthur Vining Davis had created Alcoa by the extraordinary range of his vision. He was a true builder—and, in order to feel alive, he had to remain a builder to his last moment.

That long-range vision is characteristic of all the great Money-Makers. It was characteristic of J. P. Morgan, who made his fortune by his ability to judge which industries held the potential of future growth and to finance, as well as organize, their integration into industrial giants. United States Steel is one of his monuments, as well as the monument of Andrew Carnegie whose company was the central property of that merger and who started out in life as a steelworker.

The Money-Maker's ability to defy established customs, to stand alone against storms of criticism and predictions of failure, was eloquently demonstrated by Henry Ford. Ford was a revolutionary innovator both in technology and in economics. He was the first man to discover the financial advantages of mass production—the first to use an assembly line—the first to refute in practice the theory of "class-warfare" by offering his workers an unsolicited raise in wages, higher than any union scale at the time; which he did, not for an altruistic purpose, but for the honorably rational purpose of attracting the ablest kind of labor and obtaining a higher production efficiency.

In his lifetime, Ford received no recognition of his achievements from the intellectuals who were swimming with the tide of collectivism and indulging in the "robber-barons" type of smears against all great industrialists. Such smears alleged that the men who had created this country's magnificent prosperity had done it by robbing the men who had *not* created it.

Tom M. Girdler, the last living representative of America's great era, who rose from the ranks of labor to the presidency of Republic Steel, was a special victim of the collectivist tide. An intransigent advocate and embodiment of independence, Girdler fought a heroic battle against sundry politicians and intellectuals who singled him out as the object of particularly savage attacks.

Many modern commentators of the collectivist persuasion claim that the day of the great individualist—of the independent mind—is past (and that future progress will be achieved somehow by everybody in general and nobody in particular). But if we look at the Money-Makers of the present who fought their way to success against the barrier of ever-increasing political obstacles and confiscatory taxation, we see the same essential characteristic: the independent judgment that discovers the new and pursues the untried.

"If a man of the Renaissance were alive today," writes *Fortune,* "he might find running an American corporation the most rewarding outlet for his prodigious and manifold talents. In it he could be scientist, artist, inventor, builder and statesman. . . . It would be a company created in a man's image, molded by him in every significant detail, building a product—the embodiment of his genius—that would be unique in all the world. He would gather around him extraordinary associates, selected with meticulous care, who would share his passions and his enthusiasms, who would create and build with him.

"Such a man, as it happens, does exist. He is Edwin H. Land; his company is Polaroid Corporation of Cambridge, Massachusetts, which makes the famous sixty-second camera."

Land's history is the clearest modern example of an authentic Money-Maker's role: like Edison and Westinghouse, he is an inventor-industrialist. Starting from scratch, he has made a fortune estimated at about one hundred million dollars.

The idea of a camera that would take, develop and produce finished pictures in a single operation lasting a few seconds would have been pronounced impossible by all the experts. The problems seemed insurmountable. Land solved them in six months. "I would be willing to bet," said one of his associates, "that one hundred Ph.D.s would not have been able to duplicate Land's feat in ten years of uninterrupted work."

Land encountered and withstood the opposition of the routine mentalities that greets every great innovator. "Land's revolution was at first derided by all the experts, the people who always know why a revolution cannot succeed. These experts included virtually every camera dealer in the country, every 'advanced' amateur photographer, and nearly everyone on Wall Street."

Land won, as every great innovator does when and if he is left free to win.

It is significant that many of the new millionaires made their fortunes either on new inventions or on their ability to revive old companies perishing from bad management.

One of the most interesting figures in the second group is James E. Robison, president of Indian Head Mills. A true Money-Maker in the stagnant textile industry—an industry stifled by the complex coils of protective tariffs and cotton subsidies—Robison made a fortune by buying run-down textile mills and turning them into lively, profit-making enterprises through his expert management.

His policy rests on opposing all forms of stagnation, and a swift, decisive manner of upsetting traditions or routines. *Fortune* calls him: "the advocate of the un-*status quo.*"

At a time when most businessmen are silent, evasive or apologetic about issues of political philosophy, Robison is a militant crusader for pure capitalism. He seems to be fully aware of the fundamental crisis of our age, and he is not afraid to speak.

He wrote a policy manual for Indian Head Mills, which declares: "The objective of this company is to increase the intrinsic value of the common stock"—and explains that the company is in business not "to grow bigger for the sake of size, nor to become more diversified, nor to make the most or best of anything, nor to provide jobs, have the most modern plants, the happiest customers, lead in new product development, or to achieve any other status which has no relationship to the economic use of capital.

"Any or all of these may be, from time to time, a means to our objective, but means and ends must never be confused. Indian Head Mills is in business solely to improve the inherent value of the common shareholder's equity in the company."

That this sounds shocking is a measure of the evasion permeating our cultural atmosphere: this is mere economic common sense, and no productive company can function otherwise.

In his youth, Robison was profoundly influenced by Professor Malcolm P. McNair of the Harvard Business School, who wrote: "The world's work has to be done, and people have to take responsibility for their own work and their own lives. Too much emphasis on human relations encourages people to feel sorry for themselves, makes it easier for them to slough off responsibility, to find excuses for failure, to act like children."

This passage holds a clue to the tragic situation of the Money-Makers. They are the only group of men who fully realize that "the world's work has to be done"—and they go on doing it, under a deluge of abuse, accusations and ever-growing demands. They go on, unable to defend themselves or fully to understand, knowing only that the survival of the world hangs on their unremitting effort.

They are the silent, unknown and forgotten men of our culture.

It is only the Money-Appropriator who hires personal press agents and postures in the public spotlight. It is the Money-Appropriator who flaunts his money in vulgar displays of ostentation, who craves "prestige" and notice and hangs eagerly on the fringes of "cafe society."

The Money-Maker does not care for money as such. Money, to him, is a means to an end—the means for expanding the range of his activity. Most Money-Makers are indifferent to luxury, and their manner of living is startlingly modest in relation to their wealth.

A Wall Street friend once said about Charles Allen, head of the investment banking house of Allen & Company, who has a large fortune and the simplest of wants: "Charlie has no interest in money except making it."

Not all the Money-Makers achieve enormous wealth; their success depends in large measure on the degree of freedom still remaining in their particular field. Some realize only a small fraction of their creative potential; some are never heard of.

In today's conditions, it is impossible to guess their actual number. I once asked Alan Greenspan, president of Townsend-Greenspan & Company, economic consultants, to venture an estimate on what percentage of men in our business world he would regard as authentic Money-Makers—as men of fully sovereign, independent judgment. He thought for a moment and answered, a little sadly: "On Wall Street—about five per cent; in industry—about fifteen."

It is this small, lonely minority that carries our world on its shoulders.

Loneliness is the underground to which we have condemned the Money-Maker—a bewildered loneliness that is not erased by his occasional moments of boisterous gaiety. It is the loneliness of sensing that he is the victim of some incomprehensible injustice. His coldly uncommunicative manner hides his enormous, frustrated benevolence, his childlike innocence—and his profoundly earned pride.

Toward the end of his life, Collis P. Huntington—one of the builders of the Central Pacific Railroad, a man of gigantic ability and mixed premises, who had the soul of a Money-Maker, but resorted, at times, to the methods of a Money-Appropriator—made a startling change in his manner of living. He had lived his life in Spartan austerity, contemptuous of all material luxuries and frivolities, but in his sixties he turned to a sudden, frantic orgy of extravagance, indiscriminately buying palatial residences, French furniture, real works of art and costly trash—the sort of things he had condemned his partners for buying.

Among these haphazard acquisitions, there was a painting, depicting an ancient scene, for which he paid $25,000—an action that seemed incomprehensible to his contemporaries. But here is what Huntington wrote about that painting in his autobiographical notes:

> There are seven figures in it—three cardinals of the different orders of their religion. There is an old missionary that has just returned; he is showing his scars, where his hands are cut all over; he is telling a story to these cardinals; they are dressed in luxury. One of them is playing with a dog; one is asleep; there is only one looking at him—looking at him with that kind of an expression saying what a fool you are that you should go out and suffer for the human race when we have such a good time at home. I lose the picture in the story when I look at it. I sometimes sit half an hour looking at that picture.

What story was Huntington seeing? He was seeing a lonely, unappreciated fighter. . . . He was seeing the Money-Maker, the fighter for man's survival in the jungle of inanimate matter—the man who alone remembers that the world's work has to be done.

An Answer for Businessmen

Ayn Rand

"An Answer for Businessmen" was first published on May 15, 1962, in an unidentified news magazine found among Ayn Rand's papers.

An Answer for Businessmen

Ayn Rand

If you want to save capitalism there is only one type of argument that you should adopt, the only one that has ever won in any moral issue: the argument from self-esteem. Check your premises, convince yourself of the rightness of your cause, then fight for capitalism with full, moral certainty.

The world crisis of today is a moral crisis—and nothing less than a moral revolution can resolve it: a moral revolution to sanction and complete the political achievement of the American revolution. We must fight for capitalism, not as a practical issue, not as an economic issue, but, with the most righteous pride, as a moral issue. That is what capitalism deserves, and nothing less will save it.

I should like to suggest that you begin by applying to the realm of ideas the same objective, logical, rational criteria of judgment that you apply to the realm of business. You do not judge business issues by emotional standards—do not do it in regard to ideological issues. You do not build factories by the guidance of your feelings—do not let your feelings guide your political convictions.

Don't Try to Cheat People in Business

You do not count on men's stupidity in business, you do not put out an inferior product "because people are too dumb to appreciate the best"—do not do it in political philosophy; do not endorse or propagate ideas which you know to be false, in the hope of appealing to people's fears, prejudices or ignorance. You do not cheat people in business—do not try to do it in philosophy: the so-called common man is uncommonly perceptive.

You do not doubt your own judgment in business—do not doubt it in the realm of ideology; do not let the unintelligible gibberish of the "liberal" intellectuals intimidate you or discourage you; do not conclude: "It must be deep, because I don't understand it" or "If this is what intellectual stuff is like, then all ideas are impractical nonsense." Ideas are the greatest and most crucially practical power on earth.

You do not hire men as heads of your business departments, without firsthand knowledge of the nature of their jobs and of how to judge their performance—do not do it in regard to your public relations department; learn to judge whether the stuff they are selling you is poison or not. You do not hire witch-doctors as mechanics or engineers—do not hire them as P.R.'s.

Know Your Friends and Your Enemies

Know how to tell your friends from your enemies. Know whom to support in philosophical and political issues. If you are unable to speak freely, if you are bound and gagged by the disgraceful injustice of such evils as the antitrust laws—at least, do not praise, spread or support the philosophy of your own destroyers; do not grant them the sanction of the victim. Give some thought to the possibility of establishing a civil liberties union—for businessmen.

And if you still wish to have a "social" mission or purpose—there is no greater service that you can render mankind than by fighting for your own rights and property.

Proposition 211: Lawyers Against Justice

Leonard Peikoff

From Leonard Peikoff's nationally syndicated radio talk show, Philosophy: Who Needs It, *which is broadcast live for two hours every Sunday, from 11:00 A.M. to 1:00 P.M. Pacific Time.*

Complete information on the radio show is available at the show's Web site, http://www.pwni.com, including a list of affiliate stations, how to listen to the show live on the Internet and how to listen to an archive of past broadcasts.

Proposition 211 was a California ballot initiative in 1996 which would have made all businessmen subject to litigation anytime the value of their company stock declined for any reason. (It was defeated.)

Proposition 211:
Lawyers Against Justice

Leonard Peikoff

Proposition 211—supposedly concerned with securities fraud—should properly be titled "Lawyers for Cannibalism."

This initiative would allow lawsuits to be brought against companies by shareholders who lost money trading the company's stock. Shareholders could sue without citing specific examples of fraudulent information on which they relied in buying the stock. Furthermore, individuals working for a company—directors, executives, lawyers, accountants—are to be held personally liable for the full amount of the losses plus punitive damages.

Existing law already protects shareholders against real fraud. But if Prop. 211 passes, disgruntled shareholders will be able to sue even if nobody in a company had any dealings with them, and even if nobody lied about anything. The company can be sued if it issues "recklessly" optimistic public statements, or "omits to state material facts"—and the burden of proof is on the defendants to show that their words (or non-words) did not affect the plaintiff's decision to buy stock.

In other words, businessmen can be sued into bankruptcy anytime that a stock price decreases unexpectedly.

"Proposition 211 says that either you knew your stock was going down and therefore you are a crook, or that you didn't know and therefore you're incompetent," said Lawrence Ellison, CEO of Oracle Corp. "And it says: Whether you're a crook or incompetent, we are going to take your house away. I'd rather walk through Sherwood Forest in the sixteenth century than live in a society that allows this to happen."

Investment in the stock market involves risk; those who don't like the risk can keep their money under their mattresses. But the advocates of Proposition 211 hold that small investors must have guaranteed security—security in the securities market!—which means that business executives must, somehow, provide risk-free investments for them.

It is the genius and creative effort of our great businessmen that provide small investors with the opportunity to make money. Capitalist entrepreneurs are the Atlases who carry the world on their shoulders—and attorneys such as Bill Lerach, author of Prop. 211, curse them and want them punished for that very reason.

"I am sick and tired of powerful people eroding the rights of ordinary people," says Lerach. What are these alleged rights? Not the American rights to life, liberty and pursuit of happiness, but rather the "right" to a risk-free investment at the expense of the producers who make the investment possible, i.e., the right to something for nothing.

Why do "ordinary" people have such a right? Because they are ordinary, i.e., they have no special value to offer—they are the "have nots." Why must the producers be punished? Because they do have a value, they are the "powerful" producers who create wealth. The basic idea behind Prop. 211 is the vicious creed of Marxism: sacrifice the producers to the non-producers, or the able to the needy.

Most of the high-tech companies in Silicon Valley have already been sued for securities fraud by rapacious lawyers. The vast majority of these cases, though devoid of merit, were too expensive to litigate and had to be settled out of court, at an average cost to the company of $11 million. Lerach's law firm has raked in more than $100 million, and he is brazen enough to include a provision in Prop. 211 that there can be no cap on attorney's fees!

There is no doubt that Prop. 211 would have disastrous effects on California's economy. But more than the economy is at stake here: the issue is justice. These lawyers are telling California: "You can have your businessmen and eat them, too." Californians should reply: "We have no desire to be cannibals who feed off the successful; we do not feel malicious envy toward the giants of industry, but admiration for their achievements; we are not 'little' people, we are Americans."

You can send that message to Sacramento loud and clear. Just say "No" to Prop. 211.

Warning: The FDA Can Kill You

Leonard Peikoff

This article is based on a 1996 radio broadcast which dealt with the devastating results of FDA policies on Americans' health.

Warning:
The FDA Can Kill You

Leonard Peikoff

More people have been killed by the regulations of the Food and Drug Administration than by the atomic bomb dropped on Hiroshima.

By the very nature of its regulatory function, the FDA fights against progress. Increasing FDA regulation has driven the time it takes for new drug development to its highest level ever. Drugs approved since 1990 took an average of 15 years to go from the laboratory to the pharmacy shelf (almost twice what it took in the 1960s). The price for these delays can be measured in human lives. "By a conservative estimate," says Robert Goldberg of Brandeis University's Gordon Public Policy Center, "FDA delays in allowing U.S. marketing of drugs used safely and effectively elsewhere around the world have cost the lives of at least 200,000 Americans over the past 30 years."

The FDA also causes enormous increases in cost. The average cost of developing a new drug today is $400 million, nearly half of which is the result of government regulation. Investment in research and development is reduced by the time, cost and unpredictable outcome of the FDA approval process.

Who is in fact saving and protecting our lives today, to the extent still permitted by the government? The great biochemists and private drug companies of America, who have advanced the frontiers of medical science and created an abundance of live-saving drugs. It has been estimated that modern drugs have added at least a decade to the life expectancy of people in developed countries.

Supporters of the FDA claim that the agency is necessary to ensure that new drugs are safe and effective. They usually cite the case of thalidomide, a sleeping pill that caused nearly 10,000 horrible birth defects in Europe before its side-effects were discovered in 1962. Because the FDA had not yet licensed thalidomide for use in the U.S., it is claimed that the agency prevented a similar disaster here.

In fact, the FDA had no knowledge of any harmful side-effects of thalidomide. The disaster was averted in the U.S. only because two doctors in private practice discovered that thalidomide caused the epidemic of birth defects overseas.

It is often argued that private drug companies are corrupted by their desire to make a profit, whereas the FDA can be trusted to give an objective evaluation of new drugs. This is the opposite of the truth. "Selfish greed" is what forces companies to be objective. In the long run, the only way to make money is to produce safe and effective drugs. (Those who doubt this should try to make money by selling thalidomide.) On the other hand, the FDA receives no rewards when a life-saving drug makes it to the market. The sole motivation of the bureaucrats is negative—fear of punishment if an approved drug is harmful. So they are motivated to "cover their backsides" by stalling the approval of all new drugs.

Pro-FDA forces argue that it is possible for drug companies to be negligent in looking for harmful side-effects, and/or to engage in fraud, and that consumers should be protected before these negatives occur. Therefore, the government should regulate the entire industry. It should treat all drugs and chemists as guilty until proven innocent.

Objective law requires evidence of wrong-doing in a specific case. "Preventive" law, such as government regulation, relies on arbitrary accusations of possible wrongdoing. It is a central principle of dictatorship.

Consider an analogous argument for a new government agency. It is possible for parents to raise their children badly, and even physically to abuse them. Therefore, the government should regulate child rearing. We need a PCA—a Parent and Child Administration. Any decent parent would scream that this is a blatant power grab by the government—a violation of the parents' rights. The FDA is violating the rights of drug companies, patients and doctors in just this way.

Without government regulation, who will ensure that a drug is "safe and effective"? The same people who do so now. You choose a drug based on the reputation of the drug company. And the drug company is constantly monitored by banks, insurance companies, investors and competitors. Your health is protected by your own diligence and by competent, profit-seeking biochemists, doctors and pharmacists.

This, then, is your ultimate choice: a long, pain-free life for yourself and your loved ones—or the FDA. Why not let your congressmen know your decision?

Immigration

Leonard Peikoff

"Immigration" *is based on a 1996 broadcast of* Philosophy: Who Needs It *highlighting the benefits of unrestricted immigration by those who want to earn a better life in America.*

Immigration

Leonard Peikoff

Immigrants are a godsend. As America's experience in the nineteenth century proved, immigrants raise our standard of living by bringing us their brains, talents and energy. In principle, this is still true. Nevertheless, today's politicians are falling over one another trying to devise ways to limit immigration. Such efforts are immoral, impractical and un-American.

A free country should have no immigration quotas or controls. Leaving aside criminals, enemy agents and disease carriers, our borders should be open to all. Foreigners have every right to settle here, so long as they do not violate any citizen's individual rights. No one—nor even all of us together—owns the continent as a whole.

Anti-immigrationists argue that immigrants take jobs away from Americans. The economic fallacies in this argument have been exploded many times: as long as the immigrants are self-supporting, as long as they don't consume more than they produce, they can only expand the nation's production, raise our standard of living and create better employment opportunities for all. This was the actual result in America's history.

But this points to a major difference between today's immigrants and those who came in the past. Today we are a welfare state and, increasingly, would-be parasites come across the border seeking government handouts. To that extent, therefore, immigration does seem to pose a problem: unrestricted entry by foreigners would mean a vicious injustice to Americans—the forced sacrifice of American taxpayers to support the worthless from around the globe.

What is the solution proposed by liberals and conservatives? Both would not only keep quotas on legal immigration but also devise new ways of keeping illegal immigrants out by force. Such legislation would serve only to perpetuate the root cause of the problem: the welfare state, premised on the unjust idea of need as a claim on the lives of the productive.

If it is immoral to force American taxpayers to support foreign-born parasites, it is equally immoral to force them to support native-born parasites. The moral issue is: parasitism vs. self-sufficiency, not the location or origin of the parasites.

Before the New Deal, immigrants were not promised anything by the government. Yes, they were told our streets are paved with gold. But if they did not find the gold on their own, there was no Aid to Families with Dependent Children (AFDC) to provide it. So those who came here tended to be hard-working and proud individuals. America was a magnet for those seeking the freedom to make their own way in the world. Those who thought the world owed them a living saw that it was better for them to stay home.

But the message the United States now sends is, "Come one, come all: freebies are yours for life, once you are inside our borders." Can we then blame the thousands who clamor each year to accept this invitation? Foreign parasites are merely an inevitable outgrowth of the real culprits: the growing parasitic class of Americans and the politicians who make it all possible.

Once we accept the principle of rewarding parasitism, we cannot morally deny such rewards to anyone, regardless of origin. The battle in the world today is not immigrants against natives, but parasites, foreign or domestic, against producers.

The only solution is to end parasitism as such—by phasing out or privatizing all government programs dedicated to offering something for nothing—social security, medicare and all subsidies, grants and special entitlements. And it definitely means privatizing the one government program that gives us nothing for something—the public schools.

In this country, a man has a right to pursue his own happiness, but no right to expect others to provide it for him. If he wants or needs medical care, schooling, milk or pensions, he has to pay for them himself, by his own work. Someone is paying for all these things right now and he is getting sick of doing it. For good reason.

America should once again become a haven for those, and only those, who seek to better their lives through productive work.

The Evil of "Respecting Nature"

Leonard Peikoff

The following article is based on a 1996 broadcast which dealt with the necessity of exploiting nature for human survival.

The Evil of "Respecting Nature"

Leonard Peikoff

One of the most insidious claims made today is: "It's our obligation to respect nature."

In this context, to "respect" means to "show regard or consideration" for something, and thus to refrain from interfering with it. For instance, to respect the rights of others you must "show regard or consideration" for what you are respecting, i.e., their sphere of freedom, and you must refrain from interfering with that freedom.

Consider the difference between respecting nature and respecting reality.

"Reality" is the world considered as unchangeable, as something outside man's power to alter. The law of gravity is a law of reality. If you try to defy it by leaping from the top of a skyscraper, you will die. You have to "show regard and consideration" for gravity because if you do not, you will be destroyed. You do not have to worry about interfering with gravity: you can't interfere with it. Respect for reality is recognizing that something is so, and that you have to live accordingly.

"Nature" is the world considered as a set of specific, changing and changeable things: rocks, mountains, rivers, plants, animals and human beings. As part of nature, these things undergo continuous change. They are not absolutes to which you must adapt, but facts to be recognized and dealt with.

In order to survive, you have to intervene in nature. You have to wipe out or overcome those conditions that are dangerous and create new ones that are beneficial. Why? Because you are alive.

All life, including human life, is a struggle against nature. Nature, to a living organism, is an adversary to be conquered. It is not a god to be worshipped. Man's ascent from the cave began with the recognition that nature must be turned into a means to our ends, and the end is our life.

Life is action, not stillness—aggressive self-preservation, not passivity. Everywhere we see life battling with nature, i.e., with the given.

A plant intervenes in nature. A plant does not "show regard or consideration" for the soil, or refrain from interfering with it. It thrusts its roots down to extract the chemicals and water it needs for its survival. The same is true of an animal. It will eat the roots of a tree. It will eat other animals. It takes from nature what it needs to survive. If a plant or an animal respected and refrained from interfering with nature, it would starve and die.

Animals react only to specific concretes directly confronting them and thus are capable of only a limited amount of interference in nature. If the conditions are too dry, for instance, they die. If a lethal germ spreads among them, they die in droves.

Man is the rational being, the thinker, the planner. He does not have to remain in the animal state, subjected to the whims of nature. He can and should remake the whole earth to serve the requirements of his survival. Man does what all life does, but with intelligence and foresight. If the river doesn't irrigate his land, he diverts the river. If there's too much water, he builds a dam. What governs him in this? That precious, irreplaceable value which is his life.

Living in the Southern California desert requires that we divert water for our survival. This is intervention in nature. Should we respect the water's natural place and refrain from interfering? Why? What about diseases? Was Salk wrong to discover the polio vaccine? That was interfering with nature. Vaccinating your child against polio and smallpox does not "show regard or consideration" for these viruses and bacteria that would otherwise ravage our children's bodies.

Consider what life is like in the underdeveloped nations. These nations are underdeveloped precisely because they respect nature. They don't interfere. They worship sacred cows. They don't use fertilizers or pesticides. They have no industrial pollution—only "natural" filth and dung. They have no oil drilling. They have nothing. Just unending "natural" toil, mass disease and starvation.

The idea of us respecting nature is a degenerate notion possible only to a rich civilization which takes its wealth for granted, a civilization that is allowing its intellectuals to attack the very principle that enables it to survive. Unless those intellectuals are replaced by those who respect reality and man's life, not nature, such a civilization cannot last for long.

Health Care Is Not a Right

Leonard Peikoff

Health care is a critically important business. Government control of this business means government control over your health and its requirements. This article was first delivered as a talk in 1993 during the Clinton administration's campaign to expand government regulation of health care.

Health Care Is Not a Right

Leonard Peikoff

Most people who oppose socialized medicine do so on the grounds that it is moral and well-intentioned, but impractical; i.e., it is a noble idea—which just somehow does not work. I do not agree with this approach. Of course, socialized medicine *is* impractical—it does *not* work—but I hold that it is impractical *because* it is immoral. This is not a case of noble in theory but a failure in practice; it is a case of vicious in theory and *therefore* a disaster in practice. Today, I want to focus on the moral issue at stake. So long as people believe that socialized medicine is a noble plan, there is no way to fight it. You cannot stop a noble plan—not if it really is noble. The only way you can defeat it is to unmask it—to show that it is the very opposite of noble. Then, at least, you have a fighting chance.

What is morality in this context? The American concept of it is officially stated in the Declaration of Independence. It upholds man's unalienable, individual *rights*. The term "rights," note, is a moral (not just a political) term; it tells us that a certain course of behavior is right, sanctioned, proper, a prerogative to be respected by others, not interfered with—and that anyone who violates a man's rights is: wrong, morally wrong, unsanctioned, evil.

Now, our only rights, the American viewpoint continues, are the rights to life, liberty, property, and the pursuit of happiness. That's all. According to the Founding Fathers, we are not born with the right to a trip to Disneyland, or a meal at McDonald's, or a kidney dialysis (nor with the eighteenth-century equivalent of these things). We have certain specific rights— and only these.

Why *only* these? Observe that all legitimate rights have one thing in common: they are rights to action, not to rewards from other people. The American rights impose no obligations on other people, merely the negative obligation to leave you alone. The system guarantees you the chance to work for what you want— not to be given it without effort by somebody else.

The right to life, e.g., does not mean that your neighbors have to feed and clothe you; it means you have the right to earn your food and clothes yourself, if necessary by a hard struggle, and that no one can forcibly stop your struggle for these things or steal them from you if and when you have achieved them. In other words: you have the right to act, and to keep the results of your actions, the products you make, to keep them or trade them with others, if you wish. But you have no right to the actions or products of others, except on terms to which they voluntarily agree.

To take one more example: the right to the pursuit of happiness is precisely that: the right to the *pursuit*—to a certain type of action on your part and its result—not to any guarantee that other people will make you happy—or even try to do so. Otherwise, there would be no liberty in the country: if your mere desire for something, anything, imposes a duty on other people to satisfy you, then they have no choice in their lives, no say in what they do, they have no liberty, they cannot pursue *their* happiness. Your "right" to happiness at their expense means that they become rightless serfs, i.e., your slaves. Your right to *anything* at others' expense means that they become rightless.

That is why the U.S. system defines rights as it does, strictly as the rights to action. This was the approach that made the U.S. the first truly free country in all world history—and, soon afterwards, as a result, the greatest country in history, the richest and the most powerful. It became the most powerful because its view of rights made it the most moral. It was the country of individualism and personal independence.

Today, however, we are seeing the rise of principled *immorality* in this country. We are seeing a total abandonment by the intellectuals and the politicians of the moral principles on which the U.S. was founded. We are seeing the complete destruction of the concept of rights. The original American idea has been virtually wiped out, ignored as if it had never existed. The rule now is for politicians to ignore and violate men's actual rights, while arguing about a whole list of rights never dreamed of in this country's founding documents—rights which require no earning, no effort, no action at all on the part of the recipient.

You are entitled to something, the politicians say, simply because it exists and you want or need it—period. You are entitled to be given it by the government. Where does the government get it from? What does the government have to do to private citizens—to their individual rights—to their *real* rights—in order to carry out the promise of showering free services on the people?

The answers are obvious. The newfangled rights wipe out real rights—and turn the people who actually create the goods and services involved into servants of the state. The Russians tried this exact system for many decades. Unfortunately, we have not learned from their experience. Yet the meaning of socialism (this is the right name for any government medical plan—from Medicare to managed care to the full-fledged Canadian or British system) is clearly evident in any field at all—you don't need to think of health care as a special case; it is just as apparent if the government were to proclaim a universal right to food, or to a vacation, or to a haircut. I mean: a right in the new sense: not that you are free to earn these things by your own effort and trade, but that you have a moral claim to be given these things free of charge, with no action on your part, simply as handouts from a benevolent government.

How would these alleged new rights be fulfilled? Take the simplest case: you are born with a moral right to hair care, let us say, provided by a loving government free of charge to all who want or need it. What would happen under such a moral theory?

Haircuts are free, like the air we breathe, so some people show up every day for an expensive new styling, the government pays out more and more, barbers revel in their huge new incomes, and the profession starts to grow ravenously, bald men start to come in droves for free hair implantations, a school of fancy, specialized eyebrow pluckers develops, demand continues to soar, prices continue to rise—it's all free, the government pays. The dishonest barbers are having a field day, of course—but so are the honest ones; they are working and spending like mad, trying to give every customer his heart's desire, which is a millionaire's worth of special hair care and services—the government starts to scream, the budget is out of control.

We have the solution, say the Republicans: managed hair care. Every haircut, they say, should involve not two, but three entities: the barber, as an individual who provides the haircut; the client, as an individual who receives it; and the manager, as the spokesman of a group or of society which are regarded as *above* the individual and entitled to his sacrifice—a manager, who knows relatively little about any particular case, but whose job as the collective voice is to cut costs somehow—anyhow—by giving orders backed by threats to the other two parties. Of course, the manager does not cut costs by increasing efficiency; efficiency cannot be achieved by orders and threats. He cuts costs only by subtraction—only by arbitrarily vetoing various services—only by demanding sacrifices.

It makes no difference in this kind of system whether the manager himself is or is not a barber; no decent barber would sacrifice his own creative work for the sake of becoming a bureaucrat giving orders to his colleagues; only drones and power-lusters would do it. So the principle of skill, represented by the real barbers, and the principle of client self-interest, represented by the client, are both being sacrificed to the lowest human mentalities, whose contribution to the process is the injection not of knowledge, but threats, i.e., fear. This is the only possible outcome when individualism is rejected and collectivism endorsed in its stead.

And it makes no difference in this kind of system whether the manager is nominally a private entity or a public one—whether he operates out of an HMO (a hair maintenance organization), or a haircut insurance company, or a formal Federal office. In all cases, the manager is still ultimately the government, directly or indirectly. Because it is the government which makes the power of the managers possible—it is the government which created the escalating cost-crisis to begin with, and it is the government which is methodically encouraging, rewarding and regulating the whole new collectivist managerial system.

So the hair-administrators—in Washington and wherever else—begin to manage. How do they cut costs? Directives start to erupt: we must limit the number of barbers, we must limit the time spent on haircuts, we must limit the permissible type of hair styles; the managers begin to split hairs about how many hairs a barber should be allowed to split. New computerized offices of records filled with inspectors and red tape shoot up; some barbers, it seems, are still getting too rich, they must be getting more than their fair share of the national hair, so barbers have to start applying for Certificates of Need in order to buy razors, while peer review boards are established to assess every stylist's work, both the dishonest and the overly honest alike, to make sure no one is too bad or too good or too busy or too unbusy. Etc. In the end, there are lines of wretched customers waiting for their chance to be routinely scalped by bored, hogtied haircutters some of whom remember dreamily the old days when somehow everything was so much better. End of analogy.

If this is what would happen under government-managed hair care, what else can possibly happen—it is already happening—under the idea of *health* care as a right? Health care in the modern world is a complex, scientific, technological service. How can anybody be born with a right to such a thing?

Under the American system you have a right to health care if you can pay for it, i.e., if you can earn it by your own action and effort. But nobody has the right to the services of any professional individual or group simply because he wants them and desperately needs them. The very fact that he needs these services so desperately is the proof that he had better respect the freedom, the integrity and the rights of the people who provide them.

You have a right to work, not to rob others of the fruits of their work, not to turn others into sacrificial, rightless animals laboring to fulfill your needs.

Some of you may ask here: But can people afford health care on their own? Even leaving aside the present government-inflated medical prices, the answer is: Certainly people can afford it. Where is the money coming from *right now* to pay for it all—where does the government gets its fabled unlimited money? Government is not a productive organization; it has no source of wealth other than confiscation of the citizens' wealth, through taxation, deficit financing or the like.

But, you may say, isn't it the "rich" who are really paying the costs of medical care now—the rich, not the broad bulk of the people? As has been proved time and again, there are not enough rich anywhere to make a dent in the government's costs; it is the vast middle class in the U.S. that is the only source of the kind of money that national programs like government health care require. A simple example of this was the fact that the Clinton administration's infamous program rested squarely on the backs not of Big Business, but of small businessmen who were struggling at the time merely to stay alive and in existence. Under any socialized program, it is the "little people" who do most of the paying for it—under the senseless pretext that "the people" can't afford such and such, so the government must take over. If the people of a country *truly* couldn't afford a certain service—as, e.g., in Somalia or Haiti—neither, for that very reason, could any government in that country afford it, either.

Some people can't afford medical care in the U.S. But they are necessarily a small minority in a free or even semi-free country. If they were the majority, the country would be an utter bankrupt and could not even think of a national medical program. As to this small minority, in a free country they have to rely solely on private, voluntary charity. Yes, charity, the kindness of the doctors or of the better off—charity, not right, i.e., not their right to the lives or work of others. And such charity, I may say, was always forthcoming in the past in America. The advocates of Medicaid and Medicare under President Johnson did not claim that the poor or the old in the '60s got bad care; they claimed that it was an affront for anyone to have to depend on charity.

But the fact is: You don't abolish charity by calling it something else. If a person is getting health care *for nothing*, simply because he is breathing, he is still getting charity, whether or not some politician calls it a "right." To call it a right when the recipient did not earn it is merely to compound the evil. It is charity still—though now extorted by criminal tactics of force, while hiding under a dishonest name.

As with any good or service that is provided by some specific group of men, if you try to make its possession by all a right, you thereby enslave the providers of the service, wreck the service, and end up depriving the very consumers you are supposed to be helping. To call "medical care" a right will merely enslave the doctors and thus destroy the quality of medical care in this country, as socialized medicine has done around the world, wherever it has been tried, including Canada (I was born in Canada and I know a bit about that system firsthand).

I would like to clarify further the point about socialized medicine enslaving the doctors. Let me quote here from an article I wrote a few years ago: "Medicine: The Death of a Profession." [*The Voice of Reason: Essays in Objectivist Thought*, NAL Books, © 1988 by the Estate of Ayn Rand and Leonard Peikoff.]

> In medicine, above all, the mind must be left free. Medical treatment involves countless variables and options that must be taken into account, weighed, and summed up by the doctor's mind and subconscious. Your life as a patient depends on the private, inner essence of the doctor's function: it depends on the input that enters his brain, and on the processing such input receives from him.
>
> What is being thrust now into the equation? It is not only objective medical facts any longer. Today, in one form or another, the following also has to enter that brain: "The DRG administrator [the hospital or HMO . . . "manager" . . . trying to control costs] will raise hell if I operate, but the malpractice attorney will have a field day if I don't—and my rival down the street, who heads the local PRO favors a CAT

scan in these cases, I can't afford to antagonize him, but the CON boys disagree and they won't authorize a CAT scanner for our hospital—and besides the FDA prohibits the drug I should be prescribing, even though it is widely used in Europe, and the IRS might not allow the patient a tax deduction for it, anyhow, and I can't get a specialist's advice because the latest Medicare rules prohibit a consultation with this diagnosis, and maybe I shouldn't even take this patient, he's so sick—after all, some doctors are manipulating their slate of patients, they accept only the healthiest ones, so their average costs are coming in lower than mine, and it looks bad for my staff privileges." I ask my lay audiences: Would you like your case to be treated this way—by a doctor who takes into account your objective medical needs *and* the contradictory, unintelligible demands of some ninety different state and Federal government agencies? If you were a doctor could you comply with all of it? Could you plan or work around or deal with the unknowable? But how could you not? Those agencies and their allegedly private counterparts in the HMO's and the insurance companies are real and they are rapidly gaining total power over you and your mind and your patients. In this kind of nightmare world, if and when it takes hold fully, thought is helpless; no one can decide by rational means what to do. A doctor either obeys the loudest authority—*or* he tries to sneak by unnoticed, bootlegging some good health care occasionally *or*, as so many are doing now, he simply gives up and quits the field.

Socialized medicine will finish off quality medicine in this country—because it will finish off the medical profession. It will deliver the doctors bound hands and feet to the mercies of a bureaucracy.

The only hope—for the doctors, for their patients, for all of us—is for the doctors to assert a *moral* principle. I mean: to assert their own personal individual rights—their real rights in this issue—their right to their lives, their liberty, their property, *their* pursuit of happiness. The Declaration of Independence applies to the medical profession too. We must reject the idea that doctors are slaves destined to serve others at the behest of the state.

I'd like to conclude with a sentence from Ayn Rand. Doctors, she wrote, are not servants of their patients. They are "traders, like everyone else in a free society, and they should bear that title proudly, considering the crucial importance of the services they offer."

The battle against the managed care, and every other socialist plan, in my opinion, depends on the doctors speaking out against the plan—but not only on practical grounds—rather, first of all, on *moral* grounds. The doctors must defend themselves and their own interests as a matter of solemn justice, upholding a moral principle, the first moral principle: self-preservation. The American medical profession has given this country superlative care for generations. It is time now for the country to say thank you—which it will do only if the doctors stand up and assert their own rights, their real, selfish, American rights. If they can do it, all of us will still have a chance. I hope it is not already too late.

Why Businessmen Should Be Honest:
The Argument From Rational Egoism

Edwin A. Locke and Jaana Woiceshyn

Dr. Locke and Dr. Woiceshyn first published this article in 1995 in the Journal of Organizational Behavior.

Why Businessmen Should Be Honest:
The Argument From Rational Egoism

Edwin A. Locke and Jaana Woiceshyn

You are a business owner who has just taken out a loan to manufacture a new high technology product, for which you have lucrative orders. Although you thought you could make the product to specifications, you have not been able to do so. You will not be able to meet the delivery deadline and cash is running short—so short that it is threatening the viability of the rest of your business. Things are in a critical state, but you desperately want the product to succeed. You have several options. You could tell the customers about your problems, ask for a postponement of the deadline, and hire an outside consultant to help with the product. But this will anger your customers, take time and not solve your cash-flow problem.

You could also get another bank loan by telling the bank's president that you need it to expand an old line of business. You know he will refuse more money for the new product, but he does not have to be told how you will actually use the money.

The loan will take a while to process but you need money now. You can get it from your children's college savings accounts: it would upset your wife (who helped fund the accounts) and the kids, but you do not have to tell them and can repay later. You can also borrow money from the employee pension fund. The employees do not have to know. Finally, you can ship the products even though they do not meet specs, and hope that nobody finds out right away. You can use customers' payment to pay back the various loans and worry about fixing the product later.

What should you do? Should you take the honest route or the dishonest route?

Clearly, you have to make a moral choice, but you can only do so by reference to a moral code. In this essay we will address three questions: (1) What are the main moral codes that have been accepted throughout the centuries and what are their views on honesty? (2) Why are they inadequate and what would be a rational moral code and its argument for honesty? (3) How would one apply it to the issue of businessmen being honest?

Historical Overview

Throughout history (we will confine ourselves here to the Western world) there have been only three primary moral codes. We refer to them as: cynical egoism, Christianity and secular altruism.

Cynical egoism asserts that one should do whatever one feels like, thus rejecting any objective standard for the good. The good means gratifying your desires, maximizing your personal utilities, indulging your emotions, or satisfying your wishes. In contemporary social science this view is represented by the subjective expected utility (SEU) model. It is the cost-benefit approach most commonly taught to business school students. In pop culture it is called "doing your own thing."

To apply the SEU model, the businessman in the above scenario would calculate for each alternative (the honest route and the dishonest route): the pleasure value of each outcome and the probability that each outcome would occur. The various estimates would be consciously or subconsciously combined and the alternative with the highest net value would be chosen. In our scenario, the dishonest route might well be chosen, because the businessman very much wants to succeed, and he might even get away with it. In other words, cynical egoism advocates dishonesty if one feels like it, if it helps gratify one's immediate desires, and if its cost (likelihood of getting caught) is low.

Cynical egoism has a certain plausibility because people do need to satisfy some desires in order to live successfully. However, this doctrine has been justly attacked through the ages for being an inadequate guide to moral action. For one, men could not survive even on a desert island solely on the basis of their feelings. Feelings are not tools of knowledge. Desiring something does not make it good for you. The poisonous fruit on the desert island does not turn edible by the act of wishing. As we shall see later, emotions are not psychological primaries; they are the result of one's premises (values, beliefs) which, in turn, are the result of one's thinking or lack thereof. (Rand, 1964)

Second, men could never live together successfully if they were guided only by their feelings (viz., it is OK to murder a business rival if you feel like it). A society based on competing whims would be truly a "war of all against all," consistent with Hobbes's view of man in a "state of nature." Nor is Nietzsche's solution, to sacrifice the whims of lesser men to the whims of supermen, any better; it simply adds inequality into the equation.

The problem with cynical egoism is that its advocacy of self-interest is only a pretense. Self-interest is not, in fact, a matter of following whims. To act in one's own actual interest requires that one identify the actions necessary to attain one's long-range happiness and survival and act accordingly, even if such judgments might temporarily conflict with one's immediate desires. Only rational principles offer long-range guidance for living, whether on a desert island or in a society of men.

A second moral code that has been popular in the Western world is Christianity. It argues that man should obey the moral commandments or suffer eternal damnation in the afterlife. Thus the businessman in our scenario should be honest—or else. Observe two major aspects of the Christian view of morality. First, the real benefits of morality do not occur during one's life on earth. There is an egoistic element involved, the alleged salvation of the individual soul, but this occurs after death; it is combined with the self-sacrificial obligation to serve and obey God, while on earth. Second, it is not based on reason but on mystical revelations which are to be accepted on faith. Anyone who rationally questioned the afterlife could easily become indifferent to morality and slip into cynical egoism. Christianity does come out against dishonesty ("thou shalt not steal"), but it does so as a dogma (follow God's command) rather than for any rational reason. This makes it an arbitrary moral code, divorced not only from man's nature as a rational being but from the concerns of his daily life on earth. Peikoff states (1991, p. 164): "An arbitrary claim is one for which there is no evidence, either perceptual or conceptual . . . an arbitrary claim is automatically invalidated. The rational response to such a claim is to dismiss it, without discussion, consideration or argument."

The ground for the third moral code, secular altruism, was prepared by Immanuel Kant (1960). Kant, though an ardent Christian, approached morality from an allegedly rational perspective. Most important, he removed the last vestige of egoism from the Christian view by arguing that moral virtue required the sacrifice of one's desires in the name of duty, not duty to anyone or for anything but as an end in itself. He advocated sacrifice for the sake of sacrifice. (Peikoff, 1982) It was Kant who entrenched the non-religious, duty approach in modern ethics.

Later versions of secular altruism substituted other men or society as the beneficiaries of self-sacrifice. There are several versions of the secular view. Long before Kant, Plato had advocated that man sacrifice his desires to the city-state run by philosopher kings, because they were superior judges of the proper actions men should take. Plato's basic premise was accepted by the post-Kantians. Hegel advocated the sacrifice of the self to the agents of world history. For Marx the proper recipients of sacrifice were the proletariat (i.e., Communist party), whereas for the Nazis they were the master race and the fatherland. Bentham and Mill argued that the minority must sacrifice to the majority (the greatest good for the greatest number) who arbitrarily determined the good to be whatever suited them.

Observe that the common element in all of these variants of secular altruism is that man should sacrifice his desires—that self-sacrifice is the good. This might involve sacrificing his desire to be dishonest, because others demanded honesty; but it might just as well involve sacrificing his desire to be honest, because the state or the party demanded dishonesty. For example, if the businessman worked for the Communist Party and they needed money, they might demand that he swindle the masses for the good of the state. In a semi-capitalist society such as ours, dishonesty on the part of a businessman might be viewed as moral if he gave the money to the poor. (The Christians would clearly sympathize with such an action.) In other words, secular altruism does not have a firm stand against dishonesty. Duty toward others determines whether one should be honest or not.

If man's highest virtue is the sacrifice of all desires, one has to ask: How is man to survive and achieve happiness? Maybe man should not gratify every whim, but he still needs to pursue values if he is to survive. If all values (e.g., food, shelter, career, freedom) are sacrificed, he cannot live. If no desires can be grati-fied, then happiness is impossible.

If we consider the three foregoing approaches, cynical ego-ism, Christianity and secular altruism, it is clear that they offer only two fundamental positions on morality with respect to ben-eficiary: indulge your own whims and sacrifice others, or indulge the wims of others and sacrifice yourself out of duty to God or society. Do what you want and ignore the rights of others, or do what someone else wants and ignore your own rights. In other words, do what works and feel guilty or do what's right and be inefficacious or unhappy. Overwhelmingly philosophers have argued in favor of altruism and condemned cynical egoism as immoral. A rational alternative was not available. (Even Herbert Spencer and Adam Smith favored capitalism only for altruistic and collectivistic reasons—because it was good for society as a whole.) To businessmen they say: Do your duty and be honest, even if it goes against your desires.

This conflict between cynical egoism and altruism is often experienced as a conflict between the "truly" moral (which is conventionally associated with altruism) and the practical (which is conventionally associated with cynical egoism). In the con-ventional view, it is practical to pursue your desires, because your life requires it, but such selfish action is not moral; on the other hand, sacrificing your desires is moral but not practical, because it makes happiness impossible.

To make matters worse, contemporary philosophers have even given up defending altruism, because they maintain that philosophy cannot really know anything (modern skepticism). Further, no one has been able to refute Hume's claim that you can not get an "ought" (a moral principle) from an "is" (facts about the world or man's nature); thus it is widely believed that morality is just a matter of arbitrary preference.

When conventional approaches to morality lead to these

types of conflicts, contradictions, dead ends and unanswered questions, clearly we must ask whether some serious error has been made and, therefore, whether a whole new approach to the subject is needed. We believe it is. A radically new approach to the issue of morality has been taken by Ayn Rand (see especially, Rand, 1964; Peikoff, 1991).

Ayn Rand's Theory of Rational Egoism

Ayn Rand observed that the first question to ask in the realm of morality is not: What is the good? but rather: Why does man need a code of moral principles at all? As a living being, man needs to act in specific ways to achieve the values his life requires. As a rational, volitional being, man needs conceptual guidance, i.e., moral principles, to take the appropriate action.

Man, like every living being, is faced with a fundamental alternative, that of life or death, which means: existence or non-existence. (Peikoff, 1991; Rand, 1964) The existence of every living being is conditional on a process of action; if it does not take the proper action it dies—its life goes out of existence. Inanimate matter, in contrast, faces no fundamental alternative. Its form can change, but it cannot go out of existence; no action is needed for it to continue to exist.

The need for goal-directed action, therefore, only arises for living beings. It is only to living organisms that the outcome of an action can make a fundamental difference. It is only because a living organism faces the alternative of life or death that something can be of value or disvalue to it. To quote Ayn Rand, "it is only the concept of 'Life' that makes the concept of 'Value' possible." (Rand, 1964, p. 17) Inanimate objects cannot have or pursue values or goals, because for them no outcome can be described as better or more successful than any other. (Binswanger, 1990) An organisms's life is the ultimate value or goal to which all lesser values or goals are the means. "Only self-preservation can be an ultimate goal, which serves no end beyond itself." (Peikoff, 1991, p. 211)

Man does not have any built-in, automatic code of values, i.e., instincts. He is born tabula rasa. As a rational, volitional be-ing, he has to choose his own goals, in the form of conscious purposes. (Binswanger, 1991) In order to do this, he needs to discover and validate a code of moral values, that is, a set of principles which will sustain his life long-range and make it worth sustaining (since he cannot survive on the range of the moment). If survival is the ultimate goal, then the standard for such a code must be man's life (the life proper to a rational being). The good is that which promotes man's life (i.e., physical well-being and happiness) whereas the evil is that which negates man's life. (Rand, 1964, p. 23)

It now should be clear, by implication, why egoism, in some form, must be moral. The purpose of morality is to sustain one's life. One's own life is the ultimate value each person pursues—it must be if he is to survive and achieve happiness. In other words, man must be the beneficiary of his own actions. It would be a blatant contradiction to advocate a code of morality which ne-gated the very purpose of morality—viz., the sustaining of one's life. Altruism, the doctrine that one should sacrifice one's life to others, is in essence an anti-life doctrine, a negation of morality at root. Ayn Rand has discussed this issue at great length (e.g., Rand, 1957).

There are some modern philosophers who advocate ethical theories or, more precisely, theories of virtue. However, these are not a great advance over previous theories. David Norton (1976), for example, offers a theory of ethical individualism based on a bizarre combination of Aristotle, Plato, Jung and Maslow. He claims that people are born with an innate *daimon,* an ideal of perfection, which represents their destiny, and are free to choose to fulfil or not fulfil it (that is, to actualize or not actualize their innate potentiality). This theory fails at the outset since there are no innate ideas. Sissela Bok (1989) presents a theory of lying and veracity but offers no broader theory of morality to serve as its base. She points out (correctly) that lying does the liar harm, but her ultimate argument is that lying is wrong because it is usually harmful to society. This implies that veracity is a form of social duty. Given that the good of society is the standard, however, she also acknowledges that lying can sometimes (even if not often) be for the public good. Since Bok does not defend veracity on principle, her theory gets bogged down in endless discussions of the pros and cons of lying in specific situations.

To say that man should be the beneficiary of his actions, however, is not to say how he should act. To argue in favor of egoism does not identify what particular virtues (i.e., means of achieving values) men should pursue. We have already identified the problem inherent in cynical egoism, viz., acting blindly on one's feelings. Ayn Rand's alternative to cynical egoism is rational egoism.

Reason, the faculty that integrates the material provided by the senses, is man's basic means of survival. Man has no instincts that tell him what goals to pursue and how. His sensations of pleasure and pain, while essential for his well-being, cannot guide long-range actions. Man has to survive by thinking, that is, identifying what his survival requires, planning the necessary actions and carrying them out.

If one's life is the ultimate value and reason is man's means of discovering the knowledge that his life requires, then it follows that *rationality is the highest virtue.* According to Ayn Rand, "rationality is the recognition and acceptance of reason as one's only source of knowledge, one's only judge of values and one's only guide to action." (Peikoff, 1991, p. 221) It means, for example, choosing to think (using one's volitional capacity), exerting mental effort, looking at facts without evasion, integrating sensory-perceptual observations into concepts (Rand, 1990), integrating concepts into principles, choosing long-term goals, planning how to achieve them, understanding the premises behind emotions and correcting erroneous ones, constantly learning and expanding one's knowledge, discovering cause-and-effect relationships and acting on the basis of one's conclusions. Rational egoism is Rand's alternative not only to cynical egoism but to every other moral code.

It must be emphasized that reason is not inherently opposed to emotion. Emotions are the subconscious, automatized form in which one experiences one's estimate of objects and situations in relation to one's values. For example, a businessman who gets the news from his accountant that he has suffered a serious loss for the year will feel disappointment and dissatisfaction because the P & L figures are a threat to the viability of his business which is a value to him. If he later learns that the accountant was mistaken and that he, in fact, made a sizable profit, he will feel happy and elated because he attained a valued outcome. If he has moral scruples and cheats someone to make his profit, he will feel guilty because he has violated his own code of moral values.

Thus a person who experiences conflict between a rational conviction and an emotion is actually experiencing a conflict between ideas. For example, consider a businessman who develops a new product that turns out, upon careful scrutiny by an expert subordinate, to be impractical. He grants that, in reason, the subordinate is right, but is furious with him nonetheless. Subconsciously, he may feel that the subordinate should not have "shown him up" and thereby threatened his self-esteem which is based on always being right. The clash is between the consciously acknowledged view that facts are facts and the conflicting, subconscious premise that no one should frustrate his wishes.

Ayn Rand discusses six derivative virtues which are implicit in the virtue of rationality: independence, integrity, honesty, justice, productiveness and pride. These are discussed at length elsewhere. (Peikoff, 1991) Here we will focus on honesty. "Honesty is the refusal to fake reality." (Peikoff, 1991, p. 267) It means adhering to the truth, taking facts seriously, rejecting the unreal as unreal. Thus honesty is not solely a social virtue (as is justice). It pertains most fundamentally to the relationship between man and reality. The businessman who refuses to acknowledge, despite clear evidence, that his facilities are outdated, his products uncompetitive and his cash flow inadequate, is dishonest just as the one who makes fraudulent claims to customers is dishonest. Both are trying, at the deepest level, to fake reality.

With regard to method, honesty requires a certain, active thinking process: the acknowledgement and integration of the facts relevant to a given issue, the resolution of contradictions, the seeking of new knowledge when required. Honesty also pertains to motivation. An honest man seeks knowledge because he intends to act on it, when relevant, not as a pretense. In content, the honest man does not indulge in rationalizations, evasions and does not substitute feelings or wishes for facts. (Peikoff, 1991, p. 269) In action, the honest man does not attempt to gain values by fakery or deception but by productive action and voluntary trade.

When dealing with other men, the honest man appeals to their knowledge and intelligence. The dishonest man appeals to their ignorance, their stupidity, their gullibility. He becomes a prisoner of their deluded consciousness. Their perception of reality becomes his enemy. He becomes dependent on their failure to perceive reality as a means of supporting his refusal to see it. He becomes in Ayn Rand's words, "a fool whose source of values is the fools he succeeds in fooling." (Rand, 1957, p. 945)

The fact that a dishonest man wants or desires a certain value (e.g., someone else's bank account), does not make the value rational. Wanting something which is irrational is not in one's self-interest. Rational self-interest is not a matter of gratifying all wishes; it depends on the wishes involved and their source. Wishes which clash with one's needs as a rational being are the result of false ideas which require correction, not gratification.

A businessman, for example, who feels like seizing a competitor's business by force but does not act on this wish is not thereby sacrificing himself to society. Rather, he is acting according to rational principles (e.g., individual rights) which he needs in order to live successfully. The premise underlying his wish is irrational, and it is what should be "sacrificed" (i.e., corrected) in the name of reason and egoism!

In sum, the dishonest man is one who has declared a war against reality. He has placed his wishes and desires above the truth and above objective moral principles. Such a policy cannot work; evading reality will only destroy the evader. Only honesty works; thus, no SEU calculations are needed or relevant. There can be no trade-offs, no calculations of relative gain or loss, because there can be no gain in denying reason and reality.

What, then, about the issue of lying to a hold-up man, a perennial problem in the history of ethics? Ayn Rand views honesty as an absolute but not an out-of-context absolute. Religion views virtues as dogmatic rules to be obeyed without regard to context—a view which leads inevitably to moral conflicts (viz., how do you obey the commandment "thou shalt not kill" and yet defend yourself against an aggressor?). Rational egoism rejects this duty approach to honesty and other virtues and argues that context cannot be dropped when practicing virtues. (Peikoff, 1991, pp. 275–276)

In Ayn Rand's view, honesty is a virtue because it is necessary for man to live successfully on earth. But this presupposes that he is free to seek values and to voluntarily trade them with others. The moment this freedom is taken away, honesty ceases to be a means to achieving values and becomes rather an impediment. The only way men's freedom can be taken away is by initiating physical force. Any threat or act of physical force will make it impossible to practice honesty (if one is concerned with self-preservation), such as a dictator threatening a person with jail unless he obeys the dictator's arbitrary commandments. In such situations it is fully moral, and in fact mandatory, to lie one's head off as a legitimate means of self-defense (viz., "Are you running a black-market business?" "Heck, no!"). The same is true when you are confronted by a criminal (viz., "Do you have any money in the house?" "No; it's all in the bank"). To always tell the truth to criminal men or criminal governments is not rational. It is irrational since they are the ones who are faking reality. It is also self-sacrificial since it is they who are a threat to life. Whether to lie or not to a criminal government depends on the context. The underlying principle is one's right to one's own life, which means "freedom from the initiation of force by others." The rational egoist perspective on lying is: Lying is wrong in principle, except to protect rational values. (Peikoff, 1991, p. 275)

Why should businessmen be honest? Case example:

We have shown why honesty is a rational, egoistic virtue, and thereby why dishonesty is not objectively in anyone's interest. In this section we come back to the business example presented at the beginning and will apply the principles we have discussed to the example. We will show why taking the dishonest route is contrary to the businessman's rational self-interest.

Let us begin by summarizing the principles involved with respect to business in general. To run a successful business is very difficult. It requires the most ruthlessly objective perception of reality, and constant, effective thinking to process and evaluate reams of information, which is only possible by separating the essential from the non-essential. The businessman must constantly ask himself and answer questions such as: What is the nature of my market? Who are my customers? What do they want? Am I giving it to them? What are my opportunities? What are my financial, technological, managerial and employee resources? Do I have enough? Am I using them effectively? What business am I actually in? What business should I be in? What should my business strategy be? How will circumstances change in the future? Any attempt to fake reality with respect to any of these issues is a recipe for disaster.

Now consider the case example. Let us focus first on the issue of how it will affect the businessman's thinking process to take the dishonest route. The product is, in fact, poorly made. How will he fix it if he does not focus on what *actually* is wrong with it? By pretending there is nothing wrong with it? The customer will not, in fact, willingly pay for the product as it is now. How will he keep his customers if he only *pretends* to give them what they actually want? Is he counting on them to be too stupid to see that he is not delivering what they asked for? Cash is, in fact, low. How will he fix this by taking or using money that is not his? Does he think that this "will be all right" because others do not know about it? How does he expect to get the money to pay back the unauthorized "loans"? By *hoping?*

He is counting on other people's gullibility or blindness so that he can profit from his dishonesty. In other words, he is shifting his primary focus away from the facts relevant to the conduct of his business and toward the deception of others. The more interactions he has with people, the more difficult his task becomes. To maintain his deception he has to remain consistent in the lies he tells, over time and from person to person—a difficult task, since there is no way of validating lies as there is for validating factual statements. Imagine, for example, if the businessman told one version of his story to the banker, a slightly different one to his treasurer, yet another to his customers, employees and family. Trying to keep the different versions straight in his own mind over time and when meeting new people becomes a precarious task as it is based completely on lies he wants other people to believe. This is why we said earlier that the dishonest businessman is at war with reality.

It should be clear from the above that the thinking process of the businessman will be totally distorted by taking the dishonest route. Rather than thinking about how to solve the problems in reality, he will be focused on how to fake reality so that it will *appear* that the problems have been solved. His method will be evasion rather than observation. His motive will be not to grasp the full facts so that he will *not* have to act on them. The content of his thought will consist of what he *wishes* were true rather than what is true. In dealing with others his priority will be to ensure that they do *not* perceive reality. His enemy will become: anyone (customer, relative, employee, banker) who does perceive the truth, anyone who is curious, who is careful, who is mentally alert, who takes the trouble to check the facts, who is at all conscious of what is going on in his business. These are, of course, the very qualities the businessman relies on to earn a profit. So he is committing double suicide. He is destroying his own capacity to think and counting on the cognitive incompetence of those he otherwise relies on.

Now let us move from the realm of thought to the realm of action. What would dishonest thinking lead to? By claiming to use the loan to make one product while bailing out another, the businessman would be defrauding the bank. To cover this lie, he would also have to deceive his treasurer or comptroller about the purpose of the loan, and the legal department about the bank agreement. He would also have to withhold information from his wife whose money he used, and his kids whose education he jeopardized. Further, he would have to deceive his employees about how their pension money is being invested. In addition, he would have to deceive his customers about the product and he would receive payment under false pretenses. He might also have to deceive fellow businessmen and friends about how he runs his business. Finally, he would have to deceive himself into believing that what he did was right, perhaps on the grounds that this was an "emergency situation" and that he really "wanted" to succeed. In order for the businessman to have further dealings with the bank, he would have to keep lying in order to cover up his initial fraud, and likewise with the treasurer, other employees, customers and his family.

Finally, consider the consequences of thinking and acting dishonestly. First, the network of lies would be so enormous that his mind could not retain it. Eventually, he would slip up or someone would discover one too many contradictions and, eventually, the whole edifice would collapse. Further, if the bank found out about the fraud, they could call in the loan (and even any previous loans), cut off all further business, let it be known in the banking community that this businessman was not trustworthy, and even take him to court. If the company treasurer and lawyers found out what he did and are honest, they would probably quit. And if they found out and did not quit, could *they* be trusted in any further dealings? If his family discovered what he had done, they would at the very least feel betrayed and his relationship with them could be permanently damaged. If his employees found out what he did, they could: sue, form a union, quit or take him to court—or blackmail him for a hefty pay raise. Subsequently, it will be more difficult to hire new employees, especially competent and honest ones. If his customers discover that the product does not meet specifications, they will, at the least, demand a refund, and, at worst, cut off all future dealings with him. Once all this news gets out, it will hurt his reputation with respect to his other products and make it harder to get new customers. His fellow businessmen may lose all respect for him as well. In the end, he could go bankrupt or even land in jail. But this is not *all*.

By failing to practice the virtue of honesty, the businessman abandons the other moral virtues as well because they cannot be isolated from each other. Let us consider another rational egoist virtue: productiveness, as an illustration. Productiveness is the virtue of using one's mind to create the values (material or intellectual) required to sustain one's life. In practice it means engaging in productive work (regardless of one's intellectual ability) and performing the best one can, constantly seeking better ways of doing the work. In order to produce something, whether an automobile or a scientific treatise, one has to stay focused on reality. Neither an automobile nor a scientific treatise can be useful if arbitrarily assembled. To make an automobile function as a means of transportation the manufacturer has to adhere to facts, such as laws of motion, properties of materials, and so forth. For a scientific treatise to explain facts, the scientist must adhere to the evidence. Since dishonesty means not adhering to reality, it immediately undermines productiveness. Instead of producing something of value himself, the dishonest person tries to defraud others of the products of their work, as the businessman tried to do in our example. Productiveness demands honesty, and *vice versa*. Rejecting one rational virtue means rejecting them all. (Peikoff, 1991, pp. 271–272)

It should now be obvious that a businessman who, despite *wanting* very much to succeed in making a profit, fails to adhere to the principle of honesty ends up not only by failing but by betraying everything and everyone he ever valued. In this respect he is profoundly irrational and profoundly *unselfish*. He is, in fact, destroying his own self—not only his self-esteem but his ability to live successfully.

The reader might argue that this example is exaggerated. We think not. There are businessmen who commit much more blatant frauds than this, e.g., stock and real estate swindles, Ponzi schemes. But for the sake of argument let us consider briefly a less extreme example. Consider a businessman who promised some large price reductions on a certain date but, by honest mistake, did not implement them until a week later than promised. The extra amount of money made was substantial, and he decides to take a chance at gaining the unearned. Let us further assume that there is no feasible chance of getting caught because the customers all assumed that the reductions took effect not on the order date but on the invoice date which was over a week later. Is it really so bad if he keeps the money?

The best analogy to use here is: Is it really so bad to take a little poison? It is true that you will not die from a little poison, but it will make you a little sick. Similarly, if you breach the principle of honesty, you undermine the tie between your mind and reality by changing the focus from adhering to facts to deceiving other people. Once this is done, it is not so easy to arrest the process, because you have switched from a principled approach to honesty to a pragmatic approach, viz., "I'll be honest most of the time, except when really tempted."

Resisting the desire to be dishonest, according to cynical egoism, would involve a sacrifice, because one is giving up a "selfish" desire. But an honest man would have no such desire, because he knows it would be irrational and self-destructive. A desire to be dishonest means that one has a wrong premise needing correction (e.g., "I wish reality would conform to my wishes") and that, pending such correction, one should act against the desire in accordance with one's rational judgment.

Observe one final contradiction in the dishonest man's approach to business (and to life). Even in the short term, he is implicitly counting on other people to be honest so that he can profit temporarily from his own dishonesty. Imagine, for example, if the banker in the first example said he would make the new loan and then did not, or if a worker said he would ship the product and did not, or if the customer said he would pay for the product and then failed to ante up. This dishonest businessman would be unable to get away with fraud even in the short run if everyone he dealt with were dishonest. The dishonest man is secretly counting on a double standard: dishonesty for himself and honesty for everyone else. At the deepest level he is counting on everyone else not to fake reality so that he can get away with faking it—in other words, he wants other people to make his unreality real.

To conclude, we quote Ayn Rand: "Honesty is not a social duty, not a sacrifice for the sake of others, but the most profoundly selfish virtue man can practice: his refusal to sacrifice the reality of his own existence to the deluded consciousness of others." (Rand, 1957, p. 945)

References

Binswanger, H. 1990. *The Biological Basis of Teleological Concepts,* Ayn Rand Institute Press, Marina del Rey, CA.

Binswanger, H. 1991. "Volition as cognitive self-regulation," *Organizational Behavior and Human Decision Processes,* 50, 154–178.

Bok, S. 1989. *Lying: Moral Choice in Public and Private Life,* Vintage (Random House), New York.

Kant, I. 1960. *Religion Within the Limits of Reason Alone* (Translated by T. Greene and H. Hudson), Harper & Row, New York.

Norton, D. 1976. *Personal Destinies: A Philosophy of Ethical Individualism,* Princeton University Press, Princeton, NJ.

Peikoff, L. 1982. *The Ominous Parallels,* Stein & Day, New York.

Peikoff, L. 1991. *Objectivism: The Philosophy of Ayn Rand,* Penguin Books (Dutton), New York.

Rand, A. 1957. *Atlas Shrugged,* Penguin Books (Signet), New York.

Rand, A. 1964. *The Virtue of Selfishness,* Penguin Books (Signet), New York.

Rand, A. 1990. *Introduction to Objectivist Epistemology,* Expanded 2nd ed., Meridian, New York.

Individualism: The Only Cure for Racism

Edwin A. Locke

This opinion piece was written for the Ayn Rand Institute in 1998 and published in a number of American newspapers.

Individualism:
The Only Cure for Racism

Edwin A. Locke

It is now taken as a virtual axiom that the way to cure racism is through the promulgation of racial and ethnic diversity within corporations, universities, government agencies and other institutions. The diversity movement has many facets: diversity awareness, diversity training, diversity hiring and admissions, diversity promotions and diversity accommodations (e.g., black student organizations and facilities at universities). The common feature in all these facets is: racial preference.

If diversity is the cure, however, why, instead of promoting racial harmony, has it brought racial division and conflict? The answer is not hard to discover. The unshakable fact is that you cannot cure racism with racism. To accept the diversity premise means to think in racial terms rather than in terms of individual character or merit. Taking jobs away from one group in order to compensate a second group to correct injustices caused by a third group who mistreated a fourth group at an earlier point in history (e.g., 1860) is absurd on the face of it and does not promote justice; rather, it does the opposite. Singling out one group for special favors (e.g., through affirmative action) breeds justified resentment and fuels the prejudices of real racists. People are individuals; they are not interchangeable ciphers in an amorphous collective.

Consider a more concrete, though fictional, example. Suppose that since its creation in 1936, the XYZ Corporation refused to hire redheaded men due to a quirky bias on the part of its founder. The founder now dies and an enlightened board of directors decides that something "positive" needs to be done to compensate for past injustices and announces that, henceforth, redheads will be hired on a preferential basis. Observe that: (1) this does not help the real victims—the previously excluded redheads; (2) the newly favored redheads have not been victims of discrimination in hiring, yet unfairly benefit from it; and (3) the non-redheads who are now excluded from jobs due to the redhead preference did not cause the previous discrimination and are now unfairly made victims of it. The proper solution, of course, is simply to stop discriminating based on irrelevant factors. Although redheaded bias is not a social problem, the principle does not change when you replace hair color with skin color.

The traditional and essentially correct solution to the problem of racism has always been color-blindness. But this well-intentioned principle comes at the issue negatively. The correct principle is individuality awareness. In the job sphere there are only three essential things an employer needs to know about an individual applicant: (1) Does the person have the relevant ability and knowledge (or the capacity to learn readily)? (2) Is the person willing to exert the needed effort? and (3) Does the person have good character, e.g., honesty, integrity?

It will be argued that the above view is too "idealistic" in that people often make judgments of other people based on non-essential attributes such as skin color, gender, religion, nationality and so forth. This, of course, does happen. But the solution is not to abandon the ideal but to implement it consistently. Thus, organizational training should focus not on diversity-worship but on how to objectively assess or measure ability, motivation and character in other people.

The proper alternative to diversity, that is, to focusing on the collective, is to focus on the individual and to treat each individual according to his or her own merits. Americans have always abhorred the concept of royalty, that is, granting status and privilege based on one's hereditary caste, because it contradicts the principle that what counts are the self-made characteristics possessed by each individual. Americans should abhor racism, in any form, for the same reason.

With a few heroic exceptions, such as Nucor and Cypress Semiconductor, which have defied quota pressures, business leaders (following the intellectuals) have been terror-stricken at the thought that there is any alternative to diversity. Their belief—that you can cure racism with racial quotas—is a hopeless quest with nothing but increased conflict and injustice as the end. It is time that business leaders find the courage to assert and defend the only true antidote to the problem of racism: individualism.

Wall Street Under Siege

Richard M. Salsman

This article was first published in The Intellectual Activist *in 1988.*

Wall Street Under Siege

Richard M. Salsman

In 1987 a squad of armed federal government agents burst into the offices of two prestigious Wall Street investment banks, Goldman Sachs & Company and Kidder, Peabody. The agents shoved bankers and stock traders against the walls of their offices, handcuffed them and carted them away in vans. These men had not been subpoenaed, nor had they been advised of any investigation against them. In legal terms, they were charged with violating "insider trading" laws—a practice for which one can be imprisoned, but for which the government refuses to offer a clear definition. In moral terms, these men, and many more like them, are the innocent victims of a culture laced with egalitarianism and motivated by pure envy.

They are under attack, not because they made money dishonestly, but because they made money—lots of money—*period.* They are the targets of a pervasive hostility toward capitalism, toward self-interest, toward material success. "To many," says *Business Week* magazine, "this cluster of criminal cases is simply additional evidence that this generation is callow, avaricious, materialistic and amoral." These people are being denounced and ruined precisely in proportion, not to any demonstrable fraud on their part, but to their intelligence, their ability and the magnitude of their profits.

Since 1981 the government has been engaged in a carefully calculated series of crackdowns against highly successful, and highly visible, investment bankers and stock market traders. The two handcuffing cases were open, brute demonstrations of the full meaning of that policy.

The Securities and Exchange Commission has prosecuted more than one hundred twenty-five criminal and civil cases of insider trading since 1981, far more than all the cases brought in the previous forty-seven years of securities legislation. Nearly a dozen bankers and investors have been sent to jail in the last five years, and penalties paid to the SEC in settlement of civil charges have grown every year since 1983, totaling over $150 million since 1981. This trend does not represent any sudden wave of deceit and corruption on Wall Street; rather, it indicates an aggressive desire by the SEC, the Justice Department and New York State prosecutors to wield fully the arbitrary power afforded them in the purposely ambiguous language of securities law. A 1915 survey of general corporations revealed that *90 percent* of their managers said they regularly traded on "inside" information; today, far fewer do so. Contrary to repeated assertions in the news media, it is only the egalitarian animus against insider trading, not the activity itself, that has been growing in recent years.

Prohibitions on insider trading illustrate the irrationality of non-objective law. The major statute on the subject, enacted under the Roosevelt Administration in 1933, says nothing more than that profits made from "unfair use of information which may have been obtained by a beneficial owner, director or officer by reason of his relationship to the issuer [of any securities]" must be returned to the owner of such securities. Precisely what *constitutes* "unfair use" is nowhere explained. The law—said a Presidential spokesman at the time of passage—was only a "crude rule of thumb." The SEC maintains in its prosecutions that any stock-trading based on information not publicly available is *per se* "unfair." Consequently, elastic "guidelines" are handed down periodically in court cases, often contradicting previous ones. The most scrupulous bankers and investors have no idea of what actions the law covers, and thus may not know, from one day and one deal to the next, whether their conduct will be deemed criminal until well after the fact.

One result has been a widening net of prosecution. In the 1960s the SEC made a quantum leap in expanding the "corporate insider" population by redefining the term to include people outside the corporation, such as investment bankers, lawyers and financial printers. The sheer fact that they had certain knowledge made them insiders. The SEC's targets have extended all the way to newspaper reporters, elevator operators, cab drivers and football coaches all of whom happened to come upon corporate information not accessible to the entire public.

In addition, this ambiguity disarms those charged with violating it. Not knowing what will be ruled illegal, they are easily pressured by prosecutors into entering plea-bargained admissions of guilt, and into informing on others guilty of the same indefinable crime.

The injustice is not merely that a clear definition of insider trading is lacking, but that the government makes a conscious effort to *avoid* defining it. Former SEC chairman John Shad, who initiated the explosive growth in prosecutions in 1981, said about naming a definition: "Once you get one, it doesn't take sophisticated minds long to figure out where the edges are." But it is precisely laws without "edges" that consign men to the flux of arbitrary guidelines and bureaucratic tyranny. Congressman John Dingell, chairman of the House Commerce Committee and an influential voice in the legislative debate about insider trading, says: "I see no need to define insider trading further at this time and give fertile legal minds opportunities to exploit loopholes." The protection of individual rights somehow becomes, in his view, the "exploitation of a loophole" in the laws.

By what standard, then, can investors conduct their business, if the very agency charged with enforcing securities laws refuses to name one? According to George Ball, chairman of Prudential-Bache, "the pit of your stomach will tell you what's right and what's wrong." Subjectivism and instinct, in other words, must fill the void created by the absence of objective law. Yet what happens if the "feelings" of the SEC conflict with the "feelings" of the bankers? It is clear who must be the loser in such a clash of whims.

New legislation being considered in the Senate purports to deal with the absence of a definition for insider trading—but in reality merely intensifies the problem. The Insider Trading Act of 1988 would make it a crime for anyone to "use material, non-public information" to buy or sell any security "if such person knows or is reckless in not knowing that such information has been obtained wrongfully." What is "wrongfully"? Among other descriptions in the bill, it means by "misappropriation." And what is "misappropriation"? The bill does not specify, but according to past SEC practice, "misappropriation" means, not theft, but the profitable use by an employee of information available to him through his own work. Thus, the courts would be free to consider insider information "wrongfully" obtained if it is simply information obtained by means of an insider. This would leave the SEC with basically the same arbitrary power it now has, but would make it appear more legitimate by codifying it.

Senator Alfonse D'Amato made clear his motive for introducing this bill. He noted that because in criminal cases guilt must be "beyond a reasonable doubt," he was worried that "leaving insider trading undefined risks losing convictions in jury trials." And to make it even more certain that convictions are maximized, the bill places a presumption of guilt on anyone accused of insider trading. The buyer of a stock may be later required to prove—by some impossible means—that he did not acquire it "wrongfully."

Ideological assaults upon Wall Street are not new. The securities laws that investors are being accused of violating have their origin in the Securities Exchange Act of 1934 and other legislation passed during the political witch hunts of the Great Depression. Congressional committees of that day charged that scheming stock peddlers, unscrupulous speculators and ruthless bankers had caused the crash of 1929 and the ensuing bank panics. Instead of placing the blame upon the central bank's manipulation of money and credit, upon the federal regulation of banking and upon the imposition of protectionist legislation, the investigators and the legislators made Wall Street—the hated symbol of capitalism—the scapegoat for the disasters wrought by government controls.

Today, too, the government's role in the calamitous "Black Monday" of October 1987 is being ignored. The Federal Reserve outrageously inflated the money supply from 1982 until early 1987 (largely to enable the banks to absorb Mexican and other Latin American loan defaults). Much of that easy money flowed through the banking system into the securities markets, bidding up the price of stocks. In March 1987, after five years of boom, the money-supply growth was shut off. Six months later the market crashed. Although there was momentary finger-pointing at Washington (focusing mainly on the huge federal deficits), the collapse is now widely attributed to greedy bankers, ambitious "yuppies" and computer-oriented traders.

The securities legislation of the 1930s had two primary purposes: to force companies which were issuing stock to divulge information about themselves publicly, and to restrict those who worked for corporations from personally benefiting through their "privileged positions" when trading in the stock market. These are now referred to as "full disclosure" and "insider trading" laws.

Full disclosure rules require the revelation of a considerable amount of information, including a company's financial condition, its lines of business, the extent of its investments, the number of its employees, its competitive position within its industry—and much more. The SEC has decided, for example, that an investor must disclose all holdings of 5 percent or more of any company's stock (as well as reveal his ultimate purpose in buying the stock). As reporting requirements have grown more numerous and more onerous over the years, enforcement has necessarily become ever more arbitrary. Ivan Boesky was actually given a three-year prison sentence solely for the "crime" of having bought 13 percent of Fischbach Corporation without informing the SEC. (In fact, Boesky had technically complied with the law since the shares had been purchased through several independent entities, none of which exceeded the 5 percent threshold; but the SEC ruled that because Boesky controlled those entities, he had violated the spirit of the law and deserved to be sent to prison.)

Full disclosure rules declare that the right to privacy does not exist for American business, that it has been sacrificed in the name of the "public interest" and a "better informed investor." The tacit premise is that, left to their own devices, companies will mislead and cheat potential investors. In effect, businessmen are considered guilty until proven innocent—or, more precisely, guilty with no means of objectively establishing their innocence.

Defenders of full disclosure provisions often rely on the mistaken notion of "pure and perfect competition," which holds that free competition exists only when everyone has full and in-stantaneous knowledge or "perfect information" about all phe-nomena in the economy. Absent this impossible condition, of course, government must forcibly intervene by compelling com-panies to give away valuable proprietary information.

Just as the non-objective antitrust laws arbitrarily expropri-ate the physical wealth of companies and industries that fail to fit this impossible model, so full disclosure laws expropriate the strictly intellectual efforts of businessmen in the field of finance, on the same grounds and for the same motive. As with all share-the-wealth policies, this share-the-knowledge scheme ignores entirely the method by which the item to be shared is first brought into existence. It evades the fact that knowledge is the product of the thinking of an individual human mind—that it is not the work or the property of some collective brain—that it is not the state's to "redistribute." Forcing innovators to share the products of their thinking does not provide the recipients with the capacity to think. It simply deludes the public into believing that no independent thinking is necessary in judging investments.

It is this full disclosure legislation that made possible the implementation of the even more insidious rules against insider trading. For it introduced into securities regulation the first arbi-trary distinction between "public" information and "inside," or private, information. Information that the government required be disclosed (or that was voluntarily disclosed) was considered "public"; everything else remained "inside" information. And just as the first half of the egalitarian premise maintains that all such inside information ought to be shared with those who do not have it, the second half of that premise insists that, as long as this knowledge goes unshared and remains private, no one be allowed any selfish benefit from it. Knowledge—the egalitarian de-mands—must be either given away or abandoned, but never used for private profit.

Although the statutes fail to define insider trading, what activity is the concept intended to connote? Part of the reason that the SEC has been able to conduct so aggressive a campaign against it is the common belief that insider trading represents some devious, underhanded practice by which the honest trader is cheated. "Insider trading," says one advocate of greater regulation, "is a zero-sum game. If Ivan Boesky is $50 million richer as a result of inside information, others are a total of $50 million poorer."

The presumption that insider trading constitutes theft is vigorously fostered by the SEC. In addition to the 1933 law forbidding "unfair use," the other main provision used extensively to prosecute insider trading is Rule 10(b)-5, promulgated by the SEC in 1942. Surprising to most, this rule nowhere refers to insider trading, but merely states that it is unlawful "to employ any scheme to defraud or to make any untrue statement . . . or to engage in deceptive practices in the purchase and sale of securities." While it is the government's proper function to prohibit actual fraud, the SEC has arbitrarily asserted over the years that insider trading is *inherently* fraudulent and deceptive, and therefore illegal under Rule 10(b)-5. It has claimed that if one buys a stock based on knowledge that the seller lacks, the seller has thereby been cheated.

In reality, insider trading is simply the means by which individuals honestly acquire information not widely known and put it to use in the stock market. It is no different from the opportunity that exists for men in every position to profit through specialized knowledge. For example, a doctor knows more about medicine than does the general public and will be able therefore to choose better medications, or better hospitals or better pharmaceutical stocks for his personal benefit. He is certainly not stealing from those who lack his medical knowledge. (And anyone wishing to utilize that knowledge may do so—by *paying* the doctor for his judgment.) Similarly, an "insider trader" may be the highly competent president of a company who is confident that it will make lots of money in the future—or a laboratory scientist who believes that some research in progress will prove to be profitable—or a salesman who learns of a new product line his plant will manufacture—or an investment banker whose job it is to uncover such facts, and countless others, that affect corporate profitability.

A company should be free to set the terms contractually under which employees, suppliers, etc. may or may not use proprietary information. Knowledge obtained through one's connection with a particular firm is a legitimate fringe benefit, or perquisite, of dealing with that company. Yet no corporation is legally allowed to adopt policies, even if they are broadly publicized, authorizing its insiders to trade. The same holds for the company's interest in handling information it makes available to investment bankers, law firms and financial printers. Free trade in business information is a corollary of a laissez-faire economy. If the company wants to limit access to the information it provides, it can contract to do so, and should expect to have that contract upheld by the state. Any party violating such an agreement of confidentiality should be prosecuted—for having stolen from the corporate proprietor of inside information, but *not* (as is the case nowadays) for having defrauded the "public."

(Nor are there any grounds for restricting insider trading on the basis of the fiduciary obligation of corporate officers to the shareholder. The only fundamental responsibility owed by management to the shareholder is to maximize the long-term profits of the business. If this objective requires that certain information be kept private, or if it requires that corporate insiders be given the opportunity to buy and sell the stock, then the company has every right to do so.)

The attacks against Wall Street in the 1930s and in the 1980s have in common the belief that the entire financial sector of the economy (and not merely insider trading) is essentially non-productive. Wall Street is typically regarded as, at worst, a parasite or, at best, a mere gambling casino where the "little guy" always loses against the "house." Critics regularly assert that bankers and investors make enormous sums of money without having to work for it. The intellectual effort and the virtues necessary to excel in these professions are completely ignored or misunderstood by intellectuals, politicians and journalists.

Investment bankers are devoted to finding the best ways for companies to raise money in the capital markets to finance their operations. Financing options are complex and myriad, so companies are willing to pay substantial compensation to investment bankers for their special abilities. A banker might explore, for instance, whether it is more advantageous for his client to raise $100 million by issuing bonds at a fixed or a floating rate, or by issuing common stock at the current dividend rate.

Hundreds of uncertain factors about the future, including inflation rates, interest rates, exchange rates, foreign and domestic tax implications—all must be identified and weighed by the investment banker. He must also ascertain the company's ability to pay, as determined by its product line, its management, its industry. Multiply all these variables by the hundreds of industries comprising thousands of companies manufacturing millions of products and services, all with varying financing requirements (to say nothing of the different countries, with radically different market conditions, in which they operate)—and some appreciation of the enormous skills demanded by this profession will be gained.

In addition to raising money and assessing the company's profitability and ability to repay, bankers ferret out new lines of business for companies to acquire and give advice on what businesses to sell. A manufacturer of automobiles may be advised to acquire a robotics company so that it may integrate the benefits of automation with its aging assembly line. A manufacturer of glass bottles may be convinced of the competitive onslaught of plastics, and be advised to divest and redeploy its assets into the faster growing semi-conductor business. These represent the kind of business restructurings which direct labor, machinery and money into their most productive uses. Another type of restructuring deals with effecting changes in the management and ownership of companies. Here, bankers direct financial resources into the hands of the most capable managers and companies.

The work of an investment banker consists primarily of intellectual, not physical, effort. An extensive degree of intelligence, ingenuity and dedication is required to analyze and to integrate the data of balance sheets, marketing plans, factory designs and management ability. The greatest compensation goes to bankers who can deal with the widest possible range of financial and market evidence and very quickly discover opportunities for profit.

In short, investment bankers produce value by providing information and advice to business. They make incalculable improvements in the productivity of the entire spectrum of American industry and thereby help raise everyone's standard of living.

The same is true for a narrower group of Wall Street professionals at whom special condemnation has been directed: the arbitragers (and other speculators), such as Ivan Boesky. The intense condemnation they receive should not be surprising, because arbitragers can earn fortunes by being the first to get valuable, accurate information and then instantly investing millions of dollars. Arbitrage is the business of making profits from the price discrepancies that often arise in financial markets—such as that between a stock option and the basic stock, or between a stock's present market price and the price that would reflect newly discovered data pertaining to the stock.

With the relaxation of antitrust enforcement over the last

few years, the sharp price movements sought by arbitragers often result from news that more capable investors or managers are willing to take control of a company by paying more than the existing market price of a stock. Since shareholders in companies that attract takeover bids often do not have the time, ability or inclination to gather and evaluate the necessary information, the arbitrager performs this vital function. He directs resources to their most productive uses. He helps investors weigh alternative offers and he takes on the risk in place of those investors who do not wish to bear the uncertainty during the time between the announcement and the final outcome of a takeover bid. The arbitrager also lessens price volatility in the market because he is often willing to buy a stock when it is being sold in a panic or when investors want to cash in on recent price rises. All of these facts attest to the productivity of the arbitrager.

The intrusion of insider trading prohibitions paralyzes this productivity. Most investment bankers are basically entrepreneurs, whose earnings fluctuate in direct proportion to the degree of their business's success. The nature of the business calls for entrepreneurial types, who are able to devote great energies and risk large sums of money in anticipation of reaping huge rewards. They are highly independent in their work, often moving from one firm to another, often starting, or buying, their own companies. Most investment banks understand and gladly accept such independence, recognizing that "employee loyalty to the firm" is not a mentality characteristic of these people.

The investment banker's product, which he creates and then brings to market, is his specialized knowledge. But, like any entrepreneur who develops something new, he makes the highest profits when his product gets to the marketplace first—such as when he is first to apply that knowledge to the trading of stocks. Buying and selling stocks offers him the opportunity to earn profits from his work, beyond what he receives in salaries and bonuses.

Prohibitions against insider trading, however, prevent investment bankers from cashing in on the fruits of their entrepreneurial ambition—and thereby serve to stifle that ambition. If conventional compensation is all that is available in this field, only conventional workers will be attracted to it, as the entrepreneurial individuals will head elsewhere.

The arguments against insider trading are not usually made on economic grounds. The classic presentation of its economic benefits was made more than twenty years ago by Henry G. Manne in his book *Insider Trading and the Stock Market.* He showed that insider trading makes the stock market efficient, in that it allows the price of a stock to reflect the underlying facts about the company. The price of a stock, like the price of any good, represents the market's assessment of its worth. To forbid insider trading is to forbid the communication of certain information, via changes in the price, to "outside" investors. And like any interference with a free market's price mechanism, insider trading regulations can only distort the reality of the product's true market value. Insiders indirectly bring news to the market quickly, so that the price adjusts to it today rather than next month or next year when the news, and the interpretation of its significance, becomes known to the entire public (and when the stock price would rise or fall precipitously rather than gradually).

The stock market promises liquidity—the chance to buy and sell at *some* price; it cannot (the wishes of SEC regulators notwithstanding) guarantee omniscience. "Outsiders" are not harmed by "insiders," any more than it can be said that less knowledgeable investors are harmed by the more knowledgeable. Knowledge is in *everyone's* interest—and laws that curtail one means of its dissemination are therefore detrimental to all.

The more common claim against insider trading is that it is morally unjust for some to gain more than others in the market due to their greater knowledge. William Cary, one-time chairman of the SEC, said that rules against insider trading "are not intended as a specification of particular acts or practices which constitute fraud, but rather are designed to encompass the infinite variety of devices by which undue advantage may be taken of investors and others."

To the regulators, "undue advantage" simply means that some men in the market know more than others. As in the 1930s, Wall Street is under attack today not because of any actual crooks in its midst, but because of its successful *producers.* The vilification of Wall Streeters is for their desire and capacity to make money. It is the manifestation of a hatred for the existence of unequal wealth, intelligence and ability. *This,* and not concern for any victims of actual fraud, is the primary motive behind SEC prosecutions today. *This* is the reason why not one dollar of the millions levied in fines in civil cases of insider trading has been paid to any alleged damaged party; all of the money has gone to the government.

A famous case, which ultimately went to the Supreme Court, demonstrates this perverse hierarchy of SEC concerns. In 1973 Ray Dirks, an insurance analyst for a small investment research firm, was informed that Equity Funding Corporation was fraudulently inflating revenues by forging insurance policies. The information came from a former Equity employee. Dirks alerted the SEC (Equity was a publicly traded company), but the commission doubted Dirks's claims and refused to move against the company. After months of SEC inaction, and when a public news release of the scheme seemed imminent, Dirks finally advised his clients to unload any Equity stock they held. This at last prompted the SEC to act—it proceeded to charge Dirks with "insider trading." Six years later, when the chairman of Equity had completed his jail term, Dirks was still appealing the SEC prosecution. He was not vindicated until 1983 when the Supreme Court ruled in his favor, but only because he had not "personally profited" from the information.

The root premise of full disclosure and insider trading laws is intellectual egalitarianism—the belief that the minds and the knowledge of all men must be equalized. Just as economic egalitarianism holds that material wealth should be held equally by each man, so intellectual egalitarianism holds that intelligence and knowledge, the source of material wealth, should be held equally. In fact, however, men are not equal in their ambition, their mental capacities or their knowledge—whether in the classroom, the laboratory or the stock market. Neither are men equal in their commitment to know reality. Since these facts cannot be overturned, the SEC interposes force in an attempt to reverse cause and effect, to seize wealth (the effect) from those with "unequal" ability (the cause).

The regulation of financial information represents some of the most dangerous of all economic controls because it allows intervention by force into the very process of gaining and using knowledge. Only the theory of collectivism could permit such results, whereby businessmen are viewed as public servants with no individual rights, as mere caretakers of the wealth and knowledge that ultimately belong to "society."

It is the ethics of envy that underlies the hostility heaped upon those who defy their egalitarian critics by earning huge rewards for their efforts. It is a wish to squash those who dare to succeed in pulling themselves up above the ordinary. "Ivan Boesky's consuming passion and his fatal flaw," said *Business Week,* consisted not of any dishonest or corrupt tendencies, but of "a desire to be the biggest arbitrager on Wall Street, and when he achieved that, he wanted to be bigger." Charles Lane of *The New Republic,* discussing the Gestapo-type tactics used in the handcuffing of the bankers mentioned earlier, gushed about "the sheer delight of seeing one of the superwealthy humbled by his own overwhelming greed."

However, Wall Street's alleged defenders are almost as bad as its enemies. To a man, the targets of government prosecution under the full disclosure and insider trading laws have been pitifully impotent in defending themselves. They accept the egalitarian premises of their attackers, and thereby sanction their own subjugation. At Congressional hearings last summer, Wall Street executives and lawyers called for a major expansion of the SEC's staff in order to improve the regulatory oversight of insider trading. The head of legal and regulatory affairs for the American Stock Exchange testified that "I prefer to have the law a little vague around the edges. It helps to deter the more venal."

This craven appeasement represents the low ideological caliber of today's "defenders" of capitalism. If Wall Street bankers and investors in the financial community are to survive as free and independent individuals, they must learn to assert their right to the free functioning of their own minds and to the products of their own thinking. In addition, intellectual bodyguards of reason, self-interest and laissez-faire capitalism must come to their rescue. Every effort should be made to abolish the Securities and Exchange Commission and particularly to repeal any legislation that mandates "full disclosure" and prohibits "insider trading." At the very least, Congress should be urged to do away with criminal punishment (which the proposed legislation would expand) for those activities. It is bad enough that there are civil penalties for behavior that is objectively honest and productive; it is the height of injustice for a civilized society to make this behavior subject to the kind of prison sentences that are meted out to thieves and rapists.

"Buy American" Is Un-American

Harry Binswanger

The article was first published in The Objectivist Forum *in 1987.*

"Buy American" Is Un-American

Harry Binswanger

There is good news and bad news. The good news is that despite decades of hearing from our intellectuals that we are "a sick society," America has been swept by a resurgence of patriotism. The bad news is that one group is seeking to exploit the pro-American sentiment for anti-American ends. That group includes many American businessmen (or their public-relations and advertising agencies); the campaign is "Buy American."

You have no doubt seen the public service announcements on television in which Bob Hope, Carol Channing and a parade of other celebrities each proclaim, "It matters to me!" whether or not the goods they buy are made in the U.S.A. The campaign may sound like an appeal to patriotism, but it is not. While "Buy French" might be pro-French or "Buy Islam" pro-Arab, by the very nature of America, "Buy American" is an un-American idea.

If you prefer American-made goods because you believe they are better made, or represent, in a given case, a better buy, you may be correct or mistaken, and I am not criticizing that: the basis of your choice is still *value*. Or if you enjoy the symbolism of owning an American-made product, that is certainly valid (one friend of mine prefers American cars because she grew up in Detroit and has a nostalgic attachment to "Detroit iron"). What I am concerned with is the idea that in buying American, value and symbolism aside, you are performing an act of patriotism or are helping America economically. Both ideas are false.

The "Buy American" television announcements offer no facts, arguments, or reasons. They do not attempt to *persuade* you—in the sense of changing your mind—but seek instead to manipulate your emotions. Should the manipulation fail, the movement stands ready to negate your mind directly, by forcing you to buy American. I am referring to the growing clamor in Congress for new tariffs, import quotas and sundry other trade barriers in the name of "protecting" American workers and businesses from foreign competition. Protectionism, I will show, is doubly un-American—un-American in its goal and in the coercive means employed to achieve it.

There is such a thing as "Americanism"—it's not just a chauvinistic term. If we look at what Americanism actually is, we will see that it finds proper expression in such acts as rooting for American teams in the Olympics, honoring the flag, being proud of our history, and supporting America's defense against enemy nations—but *not* in the economic nationalism of "Buy American."

What is America? America is the nation of individualism. Ayn Rand wrote, "Individualism regards man—every man—as an independent, sovereign entity who possesses an inalienable right to his own life, a right derived from his nature as a rational being." (*The Virtue of Selfishness*, p. 129) Individualism holds that each individual is an end in himself, not the means to the ends of others. It means that no group can claim any part of his life as its to dispose of—not the society, the state, the race or the nation. His personal identity, moral worth and political rights pertain to him as an individual, not as a member of any collective.

But collectivism is the premise of "Buy American." We are to think of ourselves not as individuals, but as members of a group: the nation. An individualist defines his identity according to the values he has chosen. He is a philosopher, or a computer programmer or a welder. He has a whole constellation of personal values—e.g., maybe he likes to travel, so he spends part of his income on that. As an individualist, he knows that it is his income, his choice, his life.

The collectivist defines his identity in terms of the group to which he belongs: "I am a Russian; because the Soviet state needs welders, it has assigned me to be one." Maybe he also would like to travel; but the state does not approve. So he spends his meager wages at the government store, buying whatever goods the state has decided to make available to him. As a collectivist, he regards the money he possesses as his allotment, not his income, and his life as not his own, but "Mother Russia's." The "Buy American" idea tells you to define yourself as an American, not as an individual, and to act by the standard of what is good for "the fatherland."

Frequently contained in the "Buy American" attitude is a deep-seated feeling of animosity to "*them,*" the outsiders. This attitude is the natural corollary of collectivism. An individualist feels benevolence and good will toward other individuals; a collectivist feels hatred and fear toward anyone who is not "one of us." Foreigners with their "different ways" upset him, for what is right, to him, has always meant: what the group does. But foreigners are not of the tribe; they are, in the deepest sense, alien.

Xenophobia, the fear of foreigners, is a thoroughly collectivist and un-American attitude. Xenophobia is nothing but bigotry. In principle, the idea of giving preference to American-made products over foreign-made products is the same as the idea of giving preference to products made by whites over those made by blacks. Economic nationalism is, like racism, a form of collectivism because it means judging men or their products by the group to which they belong, not by their own individual, objective attributes.

Individualism, as the quote from Ayn Rand indicates, regards man as a rational being. This implies that the interests of men are in harmony. A rational being survives and achieves his well-being by using his mind to produce material values. Collectivism regards men as irrational brutes whose interests conflict— it's a dog-eat-dog world in the collectivist view. Wealth is viewed as a static, given quantity which has to be divided up. The best chance a brute has is to cling to his group and fight all the other groups for the biggest share of the loot.

The conflicts-of-interest metaphysics has rarely been stated as bluntly as by that arch-collectivist Adolf Hitler:

> If men wish to live, then they are forced to kill others. The entire struggle for survival is a conquest of the means of existence which in turn results in the elimination of others from these same sources of subsistence. As long as there are peoples on this earth, there will be nations against nations. . . . One is either the hammer or the anvil. We confess that it is our purpose to prepare the German people again for the role of the hammer. (Quoted in *Communism, Fascism, and Democracy,* ed. by Carl Cohen, p. 410.)

This ugly metaphysics, in a milder form, is exactly the premise of the "Buy American" campaign. "It's Japan or us," they hold. "We used to have a 'favorable' balance of trade with Japan, now we have an 'unfavorable' one. This must be stopped." But notice that for us to have a favorable balance of trade, Japan must have an unfavorable one. This nonsense about the balance of trade is referred to in economics as the policy of "beggar your neighbor," the collectivist doctrine that by making your neighbor into a beggar, you profit.

Observe that this doctrine actually makes international trade of any kind impossible. For it means that every country should seek only to export and never to import. If we should buy American, then logically the Japanese should buy Japanese, the English should buy English, the Venezuelans should buy Venezuelan. The consistent result of the collectivist approach to men's interests would be universal hermitry—one should seek to avoid all contact with one's natural enemies—i.e., other men.

Where the collectivist holds that one man's gain is another man's loss, the individualist holds that one man's gain is another man's gain. What's good for General Motors is good for America. But more than that, what's good for Toyota is good for America—that's individualism and that's Amencanism.

The individualist holds that one man's ability is a value to all other men. The following fantasy example will illustrate the validity of this principle.

You rub a magic lamp, and a genie appears. He informs you that you must choose between living on either of two entirely separate worlds. In world A, everyone is stupid, clumsy, ugly, ignorant, lazy; in that world, you would be, by far, the smartest, most talented, attractive, knowledgeable, ambitious, etc. But you would not change; you would have no more of these values than you do now—only the others you are compared to would be different. In world B, you would also remain just as you are now, but everyone around you would be much smarter, more talented, and so on.

In world A, you would be a superstar—in a pool of clods, wimps, fools and ignoramuses. In world B, you would be on the bottom of all the scales, a relative nobody—in a world of gods and goddesses.

In world A, your superior ability would raise you to the top of the economic pyramid. You could have the best of everything—the best that the other producers can offer: the biggest mud hut and the largest array of animal skins. In world B, your inferior ability would leave you on the bottom of the economic pyramid. You would have to settle for a second-hand, dented matter-transporter, you would have to stop your education at the Ph.D. level and get a job as a mere assistant scientist, working a full 25-hour week just to be able to afford a month's vacation on one of the less-fashionable planets.

In world A, since medical science is unknown, your childhood would be wracked by disease, and you would die in a plague at age 25. In world B, you would live to age 350 and do so not only in perfect health, but in a body tailored to your desires by genetic engineering.

So much for the idea that you are better off when others are worse off.

Productive strength is a value to everyone. Weakness and self-defeat is not in anyone's interest, neither the weakened one's, nor that of anyone who is trading with him. It is in your interest that other men be smart, healthy, productive and free, not stupid, sick, lazy and enslaved. To take a non-fantasy example, would you be better off if Thomas Edison had been stupid, sick, lazy or enslaved? Would you be better off if the corner newsdealer were? Nothing is changed if we substitute a Japanese inventor for Thomas Edison.

Now consider the moral meaning of America. Individualism prescribes that all relations among men must be voluntary, that men must deal with each other as independent equals who cooperate for mutual benefit, neither party sacrificing the interests of the other. The moral basis of individualism is the ethics of egoism—rational selfishness. It holds that each person's life belongs to him to live as he chooses, respecting the equal right of all others to do likewise.

But "Buy American" represents the altruistic ethics of self-sacrifice. It is the demand that you buy not the product that is best for you, but one that is more expensive, lower quality or less reliable, in the name of benefitting inefficient American businessmen and workers. The ethics of self-sacrifice depends upon and reinforces the idea that men are brutes whose interests are in conflict. As Ayn Rand wrote in *The Fountainhead,* "Man was forced to accept masochism as his ideal—under the threat that sadism was his only alternative."

Where is that phony altruist cheering squad to say "All men are brothers" and "No man is an island," now, in the sense in which it is true? There is a brotherhood of men—if the men are independent, productive individuals. Man the producer is a brother to man the producer. But the professional altruists speak of brotherhood only when there is suffering and loss to be imposed, not when there is gain and pleasure.

Individualism upholds individual justice; treating each man as he objectively deserves in the light of a rational judgment of his character and actions. There is no such thing, the individualist holds, as "social justice." There is only individual justice, which requires dealing with men on the basis of what they have made of themselves, not on the basis of accidents of birth which divide them into certain racial groups, economic classes or nationalities. Justice, for the individualist, is a matter of loyalty to the facts.

Let me interject, in this regard, the following statement by an American advertising executive, which nicely captures the flavor of loyalty to the facts in regard to the issue at hand: buying American versus buying the best. He is speaking, here, about the illicit use of patriotic appeals in advertising:

> The fact that Miller Beer is "Made the American Way—born and bred in the U.S.A." is neither a legitimate nor persuasive reason to drink it. The fact that Kodak is "setting out

to find America" (in film, by the way)—even the fact that they assure me, at the end of the song, that they are "so glad to be in America"—is not a sufficient or plausible reason for me to take snapshots with Kodak film. It's nice of Wrangler to assure me that their jeans are made in the U.S.A. but it does not convince me to tear off my Sassons in tribute to Uncle Sam. If I wanted to dress for my country I'd join the Marines. (Malcolm MacDougall, *Adweek,* July 28, 1986)

Can an individualist be patriotic? Yes, if the country concerned is one meriting his allegiance. An individualist can and does value the institutions, history and laws of an individualist country. But an individualist could not be patriotic in Nazi Germany, Soviet Russia or Khomeini's Iran. This is the difference between rational patriotism and chauvinism. The chauvinist is the man who says, "My country right or wrong"; the rational patriot is the man who says, "It's my country because it's right— I live here by choice." The individualist attitude is expressed in a familiar taunt associated with patriotic New York taxi drivers: "If you don't like it here, why don't you move to Russia?" The line may not be elegant, but when addressed to collectivists, it is truly unanswerable.

The political-economic expression of individualism is capitalism—the system of private property and free trade for private profit. If Americanism means anything, it means capitalism.

Capitalism does not stop at the borders of a nation. According to individualism, man's proper relationship to man stems not from his citizenship in this or that country, but from his nature as a human being. The same principles of moral behavior apply to an American whether he is dealing with another American or a Japanese. In particular, the right of free trade applies not only within our borders, but also in our trade with foreign nations.

And in the case of America, free international trade has a special, historical meaning: America was founded for the purpose of international trade. The first permanent English settlement in America was at Jamestown, Virginia. Jamestown was founded by a multinational corporation, the London Company, for the purpose of private profit. Unlike the later Puritans, the Jamestown colonists came not for religious but for economic reasons. By 1624, when King James I dissolved it, the London Company had invested 200,000 pounds sterling and had sent more than 14,000 colonists to Virginia.

Not only was foreign trade the motive for America's first settlement, the desire for freedom of foreign trade was also one of the motives behind the establishment of American independence. Through the Sugar Act, the Townshend Acts, the Tea Act, etc., the English Parliament had forced the colonists to pay a tariff on imports and had even forbidden the colonists to buy certain goods from countries other than England. The Boston Tea Party epitomized the Americans' defiant response to these barriers to free trade.

The American Revolution was a magnificent expression of individualism. Instead of meek loyalty to the "mother country," the Founding Fathers demanded justice—and not finding it, they renounced their allegiance to England ("What signifies it to me, whether he who [invades my rights] is a king or a common man; my countryman or not my countryman?" asked Thomas Paine). The Declaration of Independence and the Constitution established a system based on the rights of the individual, a system in which the government existed to protect individual freedom, not to "protect" inefficient businesses from the people's exercise of that freedom.

In one of Jefferson's letters, he wrote: "a wise and frugal government . . . shall restrain men from injuring one another, shall leave them otherwise free to regulate their own pursuits of industry and improvement, and shall not take from the mouth of labor the bread it has earned." He did not add: "unless the wheat for that bread was imported." In another letter, he states, "The mass of mankind has not been born with saddles on their backs, nor a favored few booted and spurred ready to ride them." He did not add: "unless the favored few might otherwise be undersold by foreign competitors."

It is the freedom of capitalism that made America rich and led to a flood of immigrants to whom the streets seemed paved with gold. The American system was not fully capitalist—the connection between political freedom and economic freedom was just being grasped at the time of America's independence (Adam Smith's *Wealth of Nations* was published in 1776). But from its founding to the late-nineteenth century, the United States was as close to a perfect laissez-faire society as the world has yet seen. The spirit of capitalism animated America. America meant the self-made man and the rags-to-riches stories of Horatio Alger.

American economic freedom unleashed the productive power of men's minds. "Yankee ingenuity" it was called. A man could rise as far as his ability would take him. No class barriers, no "old wealth" could stand in the way of an Andrew Carnegie, a Henry Ford or a Thomas Edison. What was most efficient was free to win in the open marketplace.

This was *not* Social Darwinism (a European doctrine). The less fit competitors did not die, they adopted the methods pioneered by the innovators. It was the natural selection of the fittest *method* of production. By letting the less fit *businesses* die, all prospered. We did not protect the businesses making whale oil lamps from Edison's electric light, nor did the owners of the displaced businesses starve to death. We rushed to embrace the automobile, rather than clamoring, "Buy the good old horse to save the stable owners." And the stable owners became gas station owners—which was better for them as well as for the general public. The popular slogan "adapt or die" meant; produce what people want to buy, using the most efficient methods, or lose your market.

The capitalists are the men who assume the risk of deciding what to produce and how, and they are the ones who go bankrupt when surpassed by an abler competitor or left behind by the sweep of progress. It was the buggy makers, not the stable boys, who had the most to lose, in the short run, when the automobile was invented. The stable boys went to work in Ford's factories at higher wages. The buggy manufacturers adapted, painfully in some cases, or went bankrupt.

American capitalism began to recede as the individualist philosophy that had sustained it began to be supplanted by the altruism and collectivism of the Progressive movement and then the New Deal. Still, we remained the most capitalist nation in the world until sometime after World War II. For example, as late as 1940, 80 percent of American wage-earners had no income tax to pay.

Today, capitalism has been replaced by the "mixed economy," and in certain respects we are now less capitalist than other free-world nations. For instance, our antitrust laws are the world's harshest. Our regulatory agencies (such as the SEC, EPA and OSHA) interfere with business to a far greater extent than do those of other nations, and the growth of our federal spending has been far faster than that of Germany and Japan.

This is the explanation of the faster growth rate of countries like Japan, West Germany, Taiwan, Singapore and South Korea. Japan is the arch-example. The cause of Japan's greater growth rate is their greater economic freedom. In 1977 Japan's government consumed about 15 percent of their gross national product; ours consumed about 22 percent. In 1985 the figures were 16 percent for Japan and 25 percent for America. If you include the spending by our state governments and the Japanese equivalents, the 1985 figures are 18 percent for Japan, 33 percent for the U.S.

Every explanation, except the correct one, has been given for the economic rise of Japan. "Cheap labor" (which is no longer true, except compared to artificially high wages extorted by our labor unions), government encouragement, a fanatical dedication of Japanese workers to their country, and some mystically better management techniques—these are the factors alleged as the cause of Japan's ascendancy. None of these factors makes any more sense than the older idea that abundant natural resources (which Japan notably lacks) are the cause of superior productivity. The actual cause of Japan's economic progress has been freedom— especially in the form of much lower taxes on savings. Savings are the source of economic growth.

It is an undisputed, though seldom mentioned, fact that over the past two decades the Japanese saved about twice what Americans did. For instance, in 1970 gross savings in Japan amounted to 40 percent of their gross domestic product. Ours was 18 percent. In 1980 the figures were: Japan 31 percent, America again 18 percent. The highest we ever reached in the '70s was 21 percent. In that same year, Japan's savings rate was almost twice that—39 percent.

A major drain on American savings is the Social Security program. The money taken out of our paychecks for Social Security is not invested but consumed (paid out as benefits). The private, voluntary savings that Social Security displaces would have been invested—i.e., productively employed. In researching the Japanese economy for this talk, I was shocked to learn that our Social Security system is almost twenty times bigger than Japan's in relation to GNP. No wonder their savings rate has been greater than ours.

The difference in the savings rates alone would account for Japan's faster economic growth. Savings are the source of capital investment: the purchase of the machinery and tools to expand production. While our government has been, in Ayn Rand's phrase, "consuming this country's stock seed," the Japanese have been left relatively free to invest in their future.

Note also that the American industries that are losing out most markedly to the Japanese—steel and automobiles—are the very ones in which the unions, backed by government, are the most powerful: the United Steel Workers and the United Auto Workers.

The American businesses that have been losing ground to Japan should have been calling for more freedom—and occasionally some of them have. But in the main their response has been: "Shackle the Japanese, as we are shackled." They have been calling for tariffs, import quotas and every form of protectionist legislation as the answer to foreign competition. Instead of saying, "Free us up so that we can compete," they have been running to Washington, crying, "Make it illegal for Americans to buy foreign goods."

One propaganda device of these businessmen is the claim that they are all in favor of free trade—so long as it is "fair."

Let me put my answer in the strongest possible terms: in this context, *there is no such thing as "unfair" trade.* The so-called "unfairness" here is not to the buyer or to the seller but to a third party who objects. This is an act of extreme presumptuousness. A third party has no right to intervene in a transaction between a willing buyer and a willing seller—especially not when, as here, the third party's complaint is that it is unfair to him that you, the buyer, are being offered such a bargain. What is he saying, if not that he has a right to your trade, your money, your time and effort, your life? It is an approach we might expect of a medieval baron upset at someone trading with *his* serfs. That sort of feudalism is what some American businessmen and labor unions are trying to put over on you in the name of Americanism.

"It is unfair to us at Amalgamated Widget when you buy from the Japanese." The proper answer to such complaints is a venerable and very American retort which should be taken literally: "Mind your own business!"

Another protectionist ad uses the metaphor of competing "on a level playing field." It is very important to recognize that business is not a game or a sport. Economic competition is not a contest. In sports, the goals achieved—the touchdowns, home runs, knockouts—have no utilitarian value. Sports are activities whose meaning lies in the pleasure that participants and spectators derive from the process of goal-attainment itself and from the displays of excellence the challenges call forth.

In business competition, the goal is not entertainment but the production of material values that serve human life. In such a competition, all parties are winners in the long run. When a foreign firm can out-produce an American one, it is to America's interest that the foreign firm "win" their competition.

The metaphor of "a level playing field" has no meaning in business—unless it means an open marketplace without force or fraud, where all compete under conditions of free trade by voluntary consent. But open competition is precisely what the level-fielders are against. They want to hobble the foreign runners in the race, to hobble them either by force (tariffs) or fraud (conning Amencans into believing that buying foreign products damages our economy).

Note the power of the connotation of words. The Japanese are engaging in "dumping," we are told. But what is being "dumped" on us is not garbage but inexpensive, high quality products. Their dumping consists of discounting the price below what you would have to pay for American products. This is also known as "underselling" and is considered a big plus when done domestically by American businesses. How many commercials have you heard that say "we are cheapest," "we will beat any offer," "guaranteed lowest price," etc? They are "dumping" savings on us. The "dumping" actually consists of showering us with wealth.

In theory, "dumping" implies selling below cost, with the "dumper's" government making up the loss by subsidies. Japan's government is frequently charged with engaging in such practices. Personally, I doubt that the Japanese government would be so irrational as to subsidize their businesses to sell products at a loss. But governments can be very irrational, so let's suppose that it happens on a given occasion. What then should be our response to this practice? If and when the Japanese are actually "dumping," it means that Japanese citizens are being taxed to give us a gift. Is gift-giving to be declared a threat? It is true that this gift is disadvantageous to American firms selling the product in competition with foreign subsidized companies, and this is hard on them. But so what? By what right do they seek to pass laws to keep us from receiving this gift? By what right would they force us to buy from them?

If a Japanese competitor is being subsidized by its government to sell here below cost, then American businesses should appeal to the direct victims of the Japanese policy: the Japanese taxpayers. Let them take their "stop the dumping" campaign to Japan and urge Japanese taxpayers to vote down the policy of taxing themselves to give gifts to the American public.

Ending such subsidies would in fact be in the interest of both countries. If a foreign government adopts such an irrational policy, we should not bar Americans from taking the gift, but the policy *is* irrational, and in the long run it is not in either country's self-interest. It is obviously not in a foreign country's self-interest to tax themselves for the benefit of Americans. But it is also not in America's interest that our trading partners weaken themselves by acts of economic self-sacrifice.

I have argued that the "Buy American" campaign reflects a false and very un-American philosophy: collectivism. Now let us turn to the basic economic fallacy in that campaign.

Economics teaches that international trade is a form of cooperation, a means of expanding worldwide production, and that the benefits of trade accrue to both countries, even if one country is more efficient in production than the other across the board. This is the lesson of the economic principle known as the law of comparative advantage.

To illustrate the law of comparative advantage, consider the production of two goods, computers and clothing, here and in Japan. Suppose, for the sake of argument, that the worst fears of the "Buy American" crowd are true in this case: Japan can make both computers and clothing far more cheaply than we can. Let us say that Japan has a two-to-one advantage over us in clothing manufacturing (it costs them half what it costs us to make the same item of clothing); and suppose that Japan enjoys a three-to-one advantage in computer manufacturing (their costs are one-third ours).

Although the Japanese would have an *absolute* advantage in the production of both computers and clothing, we would have a *comparative* advantage in the production of clothing. The law of comparative advantage holds that both countries benefit when each specializes in the production of the goods in which it has a comparative advantage. Here, both countries would benefit if Japan specialized in computers and we specialized in clothing and then traded some of our clothing for their computers.

The benefits gained do not depend upon the fact that specialization tends to reduce costs (e.g., through economies of scale). Rather, the gains follow from the fact that worldwide production is expanded when each country devotes its resources to those activities in which it is relatively more productive. In my example, even though I assumed that the Japanese can make clothing more cheaply than we can, by leaving the clothing manufacturing to us they free up resources to expand their computer production, where their relative efficiency is greater. Then they trade some of the extra computers the specialization has enabled them to produce for some of our similarly expanded clothing production.

The law of comparative advantage can be demonstrated mathematically (see any economics text), but it is often illustrated more simply by the following example. Suppose a certain executive knows that he can type and file faster than his secretary. Nonetheless, it pays him to leave the secretarial work to her. Why? Because her work gives him extra time to devote to his area of comparative advantage—running the company. As an executive, his time is worth, say, $100 an hour; it is too valuable to waste in doing secretarial work worth only $10 an hour, even though he could do that work more efficiently than his secretary. In the same way, in the preceding example, Japan's computer-producing time is worth too much to waste in manufacturing clothing, even though the Japanese can manufacture clothing more cheaply than we can.

The law of comparative advantage is hardly a recent discovery. It was identified in 1817 by David Ricardo and is accepted by virtually all economists today. One of the most popular texts in economics is Paul Samuelson's *Economics*. Samuelson, a Kennedy-style liberal, states the principle thus: "Whether or not one of two regions is absolutely more efficient in the production of every good than is the other, if each specializes in the products in which it has a *comparative advantage* (greatest *relative* efficiency), trade will be mutually profitable to both regions." He goes on to note that such specialization is beneficial to workers, leading to a rise in real wages in both regions.

Samuelson also enters a significant qualification to the law's applicability: "The theory disregards all stickiness of prices and wages, all transitional inflationary and deflationary gaps, and all balance-of-payments problems. It pretends that when workers go out of one industry they always go into another more efficient industry—never into chronic unemployment." Though Samuelson does not say so, what this means is that the advantages of international trade depend upon domestic freedom. For what causes "stickiness of prices and wages," "inflation," and "chronic unemployment"? Government interference in the free market. Prices only "stick" when government controls, such as price controls, prevent businesses from adjusting prices to market conditions. Wages in an industry "stick" only when labor unions, backed by government power, prevent them from falling (for example, the wages in the American auto industry are not just "sticky," they are riveted to uneconomic levels, courtesy of the political power of the United Autoworkers Union). Inflation and deflation are caused by the government's control of the money supply. And chronic unemployment is due to union power plus the minimum wage law.

When the "Buy American" crowd demands that you pay more for your products, lowering your standard of living or working harder to maintain it, there are profiteers: your sacrifices support the parasitism of the unions. Having extorted wage rates higher than a free market would support, having caused the products in their industries to be priced out of the international market, the unions respond with the demand that the market be closed. Even less appetizing are the Orren Boyle-type [a character in Ayn Rand's *Atlas Shrugged*] mixed-economy businessmen who flourish under controls. Their political pull gives them a coercive grip on domestic markets, which amounts to a legalized license to pick our pockets.

Professor Samuelson concludes his discussion of the law of comparative advantage, despite his demurrals, with this verdict:

> Political economy has found few more pregnant principles. A nation that neglects comparative advantage may have to pay a heavy price in terms of living standards and potential rates of growth. . . . From the standpoint of pure economic welfare, the slogan, "Buy American" is as foolish as would be "Buy Wisconsin," or "Buy Oshkosh, Wisconsin," or "Buy South Oshkosh, Wisconsin." Part of our great prosperity has come from the fortunate fact that there have been no restric-

tive customs duties within our vast fifty states, and we have formed a great free-trade area.

The law of comparative advantage applies not only to international trade but to all trade. It is a concretization, in the realm of economics, of the philosophic principle that the rational interests of all men are in harmony. Trade is the exchange of values, and it occurs when each party judges that he will benefit from the exchange. In trade, one man's gain is another man's gain. A trade, in this context, is not a gift or an act of self-sacrifice; the premise of trade is mutual self-interest. And it is not trade but theft or extortion if one party gains possession of another's goods without his free consent. When do traders give their free consent? When each prefers what he is being offered to what he has to give in exchange—i.e., when each judges that he will gain by the transaction.

The essence of the answer to protectionism lies in recognizing the life-and-death difference between economic competition and physical conflict. Economic competition is a rivalry in producing and offering values: it is ultimately a form of cooperation under the division of labor. Physical conflict is a destructive form of opposition in which at least one party must lose. It is the difference between economic power and the power of physical force. The equivocation between these two, between the dollar and the gun, is the main weapon of the Marxists. Marx claimed that economic power, the offering of values in trade, is "capitalist exploitation." Lenin called it "imperialism." Are we to fall into the Marxist-Leninist trap of regarding the products of our allies as "economic imperialism" that "exploits" us? Are we to buy communism in the name of buying American?

We are in competition with Japan; we are in physical conflict with Soviet Russia. For the same reasons that it is morally proper to trade with the Japanese, it is morally wrong to trade with Soviet Russia. "Don't buy communist goods" *is* a properly American, patriotic attitude. The Soviet Union and the United States are not trading partners but enemies. I said earlier that what's good for Toyota is good for America. But what's good for the Politburo is bad for America: the Politburo defines its interest as lying in our enslavement. It is revealing of the sad state of our intellectual leadership that there is more concern in this country with limiting trade with free-world nations like Japan than with slave-states like Russia.

I said that we are in competition with Japan. It would be more accurate to say that some American firms compete with some Japanese firms. GM competes with Toyota, but GM does not compete with Japanese computer-chip makers—in fact, GM buys these chips for its cars. Exxon does not compete with Toyota—in fact, if Americans buy Toyotas instead of more expensive American cars, some of the money we save can be spent on buying Exxon's gasoline.

Every improvement in Japan's production is good for some U.S. firms and bad (in the short run) for others. But it is impossible for Japan's growth to be bad on net balance for America, even if Japan grows faster than we do across the board in every industry. What counts is the progress in production that is made, not which country makes it faster. If the Japanese improve across the board, that means that Americans can get all Japanese products more cheaply. The money saved on these purchases is then available to buy more American goods and to invest in expanding American production.

In general, anything that facilitates another's productivity is good for all those who trade with him. The value another man produces is what he has to offer you in exchange. Money is just the medium of exchange. Ignoring this simple fact is what gives rise to the popular worries about our so-called "balance of trade problem."

The headlines are blaring alarms about the dire consequence of our "trade deficit" and the "unfavorable balance of trade" which we supposedly have with countries like Japan. What is this all about? The dollar value of our imports exceeds the dollar value of our exports. So what? The United States had this kind of "trade deficit" practically every year of the nineteenth century—the period of our fastest economic growth.

Worry about "trade deficits" reflects a bias in favor of exports over imports, an attitude harking back to mercantilist fallacies of the sixteenth and seventeenth centuries. This import-phobia represents a perverse confusion of wealth and money. Imports are actual goods coming into the country. What goes to foreigners is the money, which in today's context means pieces of paper. Thus, the fear of the "trade deficit" represented by "excessive" imports amounts to a fear of too many goods coming into the country and too few being taken out by foreigners.

That's the issue from the side of goods. When we consider it from the side of dollar bills, the absurdity of the fear of "trade deficits" becomes even more apparent. We pay for foreign goods, such as Toyotas, with American dollars. Even if an American travels to Japan and buys a Toyota there with yen, to get the yen he had to exchange dollars for yen, so he still, indirectly, pays for the Toyota with dollars. And dollars can be spent only in America. Any foreigner who accepts dollars in payment for his goods does so only because he intends to spend those dollars here—or to trade them with someone who in turn intends to spend them here. There is nothing else to do with dollars. Their only value is as a demand for American goods and services—aside from that, they are just paper. This means that in the last analysis a trade imbalance is but a short-range, bookkeeping artifact. A real, long-term trade imbalance would require that the Japanese give us Toyotas for dollars which they then throw in the trash.

What then is the meaning of the trade imbalance statistics

reported in the media? This nominal "imbalance" is actually a sign of America's economic strength: it reflects net foreign investment in our economy. Foreign exporters have been using some of their dollar earnings to buy American stocks, bonds and real estate. The balance of trade figures, however, do not include these capital expenditures by foreigners. In other words, when an American buys a Toyota for $10,000, if Toyota uses those dollars to buy IBM shares on the stock market—or just leaves them in an American bank to draw interest—a $10,000 trade "deficit" automatically appears on the balance sheet.

In a very real sense, such an investment-produced trade "imbalance" is something we should welcome: the alternative use of that $10,000 is to buy American products—in which case there would be fewer American products available to American buyers; the Japanese would be bidding against us for the purchase of our output. As it is, however, the trade "deficit" marks the extent to which the Japanese supply us with goods (e.g., Toyotas) while deferring their reward for doing so instead turning over the dollar equivalent of their reward to our capital markets to expand our economy. Not only do we get Japanese cars and stereos without having to part immediately with some of our wheat, oil, etc., but we get the use of those dollars in the meantime.

Another way in which the dollars spent on foreign imports have been repatriated is through the purchase of American assets. You probably have seen the reports in the media about Japanese purchases of American real estate. In Waikiki, almost all of the beachfront hotels have been bought by Japanese investors. Japanese-held dollars have also been used to purchase New York office buildings and Texas ranch land. And the Japanese have been investing in American automobile factories in the South and Midwest. This is the direct and beneficial consequence of the so-called trade imbalance.

A very significant repatriation of our dollars, and one that is also not included in the trade accounts, is foreign purchases of our government bonds. If you have wondered why our huge budget deficits have not wreaked more visible damage upon our economy, this is a major part of the answer: foreigners have been purchasing U.S. treasury bills—i.e., they have been loaning us the money to finance our budget deficits. Without foreign purchases of our government bonds, we would have experienced in the '80s either a severe inflation or a credit collapse (or both). Thus, it is no exaggeration to say that it is our trade "deficit" that has kept our economy afloat throughout this decade.

I have argued that the fear of foreign competition is as irrational as the fear of domestic competition, and that the proper attitude for all concerned, even the "losers" of the competition, is "let the better man win"—that way all actually win because the rational interests of men are in harmony.

Supporting less efficient producers merely because they live in this country means sacrificing your economic self-interest to theirs and sacrificing the interests of those who would have profited from the money you could have saved by buying a cheaper import. It means, in short, acting unjustly: protecting incompetence at the expense of competence.

Government interference with free trade is un-American. Sacrificing one's own standard of living to subsidize inefficient producers is un-American. The tribal fear of foreigners is un-American.

And for all these reasons, "Buy American" is un-American. A patriotic American acts as a capitalist and an individualist: he buys the best. America will again lead the world in economic growth when we re-institute its cause: freedom.

.

The Dollar and the Gun

Harry Binswanger

This article was first published in The Objectivist Forum *in 1983.*

The Dollar and the Gun

Harry Binswanger

To advocates of capitalism, the following scenario is all too familiar.

You are in a conversation with an acquaintance. The conversation turns to politics. You make it clear you are for capitalism, laissez-faire capitalism. Eloquently, you explain the case for capitalism in terms of man's rights, the banning of physical force and the limitation of government to the function of protecting individual freedom. It seems clear, simple, unanswerable.

But instead of seeing the "light-bulb look" on the face of your acquaintance, you see shock, bewilderment, antagonism. At the first opportunity, he rushes to object:

"But government has to protect helpless consumers from the power wielded by huge multinational corporations."

Or: "Freedom is impossible under strict capitalism: people must have jobs in order to live, and they are therefore forced to accept the employer's terms."

Or: "In a complex industrial society such as ours, government planning must replace the anarchy of the marketplace."

These apparently diverse objections all commit the same logical fallacy, a fallacy grounded in the deepest philosophical premises of those who commit it. To defend capitalism effectively, one must be able to recognize and combat this fallacy in whatever form it may appear. The fallacy is equivocation—the equivocation between economic power and political power.

"Political power" refers to the power of government. The special nature of that power is what differentiates government from all other social institutions. That which makes government government, its essential attribute, is its monopoly on the use of physical force. Only a government can make *laws*—i.e., rules of social conduct backed up by physical force. A "government" lacking the power to use force is not a government at all, but some sort of ugly pretense, like the United Nations.

A non-governmental organization can make rules, pass resolutions, etc., but these are not laws precisely because they cannot be enforced on those who choose not to deal with that organization. The penalty for breaking the rules of, e.g., a fraternal organization is expulsion from the association. The penalty for breaking the law is fines, imprisonment, and ultimately, death. The symbol of political power is a gun.

A proper government points that gun only at those who violate individual rights, to answer the physical force they have initiated, but it is a gun nonetheless.

Economic power, on the other hand, is the ability to produce material values and offer them for sale. E.g., the power of Big Oil is the power to discover, drill and bring to market a large amount of oil. Economic power lies in assets—i.e., the factors of production, the inventory and the cash possessed by businesses. The symbol of economic power is the dollar.

A business can only make you an offer, thereby expanding

the possibilities open to you. The alternative a business presents you with in a free market is: "Increase your well-being by trading with us, or go your own way." The alternative a government, or any force-user, presents you with is: "Do as we order, or forfeit your liberty, property or life."

As Ayn Rand wrote, "economic power is exercised by means of a *positive*, by offering men a reward, an incentive, a payment, a value; political power is exercised by means of a *negative*, by the threat of punishment, injury, imprisonment, destruction. The businessman's tool is *values*; the bureaucrat's tool is *fear*." (*Capitalism: The Unknown Ideal*, p. 48)

Economic power stems from and depends upon the voluntary choices of the buying public. *We* are the ones who make big businesses big. One grants economic power to a company whenever one buys its products. And the reason one buys is to profit by the purchase: one values the product more than the money it costs—otherwise, one would not buy it. (The savage polemics against the profits of business are demands that the entire gain should go to one side—that "the little guy" should get all of the gain and businesses none, rather than both profiting from the transaction.)

To the extent a business fails at producing things people choose to buy, it is powerless. The mightiest Big Multinational Conglomerate which devoted its power to producing items of no value would achieve no effect other than its own bankruptcy.

Economic power, then, is purely benevolent. It does not include the power to harm people, enslave them, exploit them or "rip them off." Marx to the contrary notwithstanding, the only means of *exploiting* someone is by using physical force—i.e., by employing the principle of political power.

The equivocation between economic and political power attacks capitalism from both sides. On the one hand, it blackens the legitimate, peaceful, self-interested activities of traders on a free market by equating these activities with the predatory actions of criminals and tyrannical governments. For example, the "power of huge multinational corporations" is thought of as the power to rob the public and to coerce employees. Accepting the equivocation leads one to conclude that government intervention in the economy is necessary to the protection of our freedom against economic power.

On the other hand, the equivocation whitewashes the interventionist actions of government by equating them with the benevolent, productive actions of businesses and private individuals. For example, when the government attempts to substitute arbitrary bureaucratic edicts for the intricately coordinated plans of individuals and businesses, this is referred to as "planning." The systematic destruction of your savings through legalized counterfeiting is styled "managing" the money supply. Antitrust laws, which make it illegal to become too effective a competitor, are held necessary to preserve "free competition." Socialist dictatorship is spoken of as "economic democracy."

Americans have always held individual rights and freedom to be sacred and have looked with proper suspicion upon the power of government. The opponents of freedom have flopped grandly whenever their true colors have been perceived by the American public (e.g., the McGovern campaign). The victories of the statists have required camouflage. The equivocation between economic and political power, by reversing the meaning of all the crucial political concepts, has been essential to the spread of anti-capitalism in this country.

The demagogic, rabble-rousing attacks on "Big Business" are the most direct example of the equivocation in practice. Whether it is multinational corporations or conglomerates or monopolies or "oligopolies," the fear of "concentrations of economic power" is the theme played upon in endless variations by the left. The anti-bigness theme often appeals to the "conservatives" as well; the first serious breach of American capitalism, the Sherman Antitrust Act of 1890, was and is supported by conservatives. Senator Sherman's rationale for the Act is a classic case of the equivocation: "If the concerted powers of [a business] combination are intrusted to a single man, *it is a kingly prerogative* inconsistent with our form of government." (emphasis added)

In today's depressed economy where "obscene profits" have turned into (lovely?) losses, the anti-business theme is being played in a new key: the target has shifted to foreign businesses. The equation of the dollar and the gun remains however. To wit: "Senator Paul Tsongas (D-Massachusetts) believes that the high-technology challenge from Japan is as serious to the United State's long-term security as the defense threat posed by the Soviet Union." (*Infoworld*, May 30, 1983)

The Soviet Union threatens us with nuclear annihilation. The Japanese "threaten" us with the opportunity to buy cheap, reliable computer parts.

One could point out that the law of comparative advantage, a cornerstone of economic science, dictates that one country's superior productive ability can only benefit all those with whom it trades, that if Japanese firms can produce computer parts at lower cost than U.S. firms can, then our firms will necessarily have a comparative advantage in some other area of production, that any government intervention to protect some U.S. firms from foreign competition sacrifices other U.S. firms and the public at large to inefficiency, lowering our standard of living. But all this would be lost on the kind of mentality that equates imports with bombs.

Anti-capitalists go through the most elaborate intellectual contortions to obscure the difference between economic power and political power. For example, George Will, a popular columnist often mistaken for a pro-capitalist, announces that we must abandon the distinction because "any economic arrangement is, by definition, a political arrangement." He attacks the idea that "only people produce wealth; government does not" on the grounds that "Government produces the infrastructure of society—legal, physical, educational—...that is a precondition for the production of wealth." (*The New Republic*, May 9, 1983)

It is true that laws protecting rights are a precondition for the production of wealth, but a precondition of production is not production. In enforcing proper laws, the government does not produce anything—it merely *protects* the productive activities performed by private individuals. Guns cannot create wealth. When a policeman prevents a mugger from stealing your wallet, no value is created; you are left intact, but no better off.

The absence of a loss is not a gain. Ignoring that simple fact is involved in the attempt to portray the government's gun as a positive, creative factor. For instance, tax relief is viewed as if it were government encouragement. In reality, tax breaks for schools, churches, homeowners, etc. are reduced penalties, not support. But socialist Michael Harrington writes:

> The Internal Revenue Code is a perverse welfare system that hands out $77 billion a year, primarily to the rich. The special treatment accorded to capital gains results in an annual government benefit of $14 billion for high rollers on the stock exchange. (*Saturday Review*, November 1972)

Harrington equates being forced to surrender to the IRS one-quarter of your earnings (the tax rate for capital gains), with being given a positive benefit by the government. After all, the IRS could have taken it all.

Just as the absence of a loss is not a gain, so the absence of a gain is not a loss. When government handouts are reduced, that is not "balancing the budget on the backs of the poor"—it is a reduction in the extent to which the poor are balanced on the backs of the rest of us.

The distinction between economic power and political

power—seemingly self-evident—is in fact premised upon an entire philosophic framework. It requires, above all, two principles: (1) that wealth is produced by individual thought and effort, and (2) that man is an end in himself.

From the standpoint of today's philosophy, which denies both premises, the equation of economic power and political power is not a fallacy but a logically necessary conclusion.

In regard to the first premise, the dominant view today is that "the goods are here." This attitude comes in several variants, and most people switch freely among them, but in every case the result is the idea that economic power is not earned.

In one variant, the production of wealth is evaded altogether; wealth is viewed as a static quantity, which can only change hands. On this view, one man's enrichment is inevitably at the price of another's impoverishment, and economic power is necessarily obtained at others' expense.

For example: in a full-page advertisement run last year in the *New York Times*, a pornographic magazine promoted its series of articles on "Big Oil: The Rape of Free Enterprise." The ad charged "the oil companies have a vise-like grip on the production and distribution of oil and natural gas—and set the market prices. These giants also own vast holdings of coal and uranium. ... we're over a barrel—and it's an oil barrel." (January 25, 1982)

Despite the ad's use of the word "production," the language conveys the impression that barrels of oil, stockpiles of gas, coal and uranium are not produced, that they were just lying around until—somehow—those demonic giants seized them in their "vise-like grip." The truth is that finding, extracting, refining, delivering and storing oil and other energy sources is such an enormous undertaking that companies too small to be known to the general public spend more than $100 million *each* on these tasks annually.

The notion that wealth is a static quantity overlooks one

telling detail: the whole of human history. If wealth only shifted hands, if one man's gain were always at the price of another's loss, then man could never have risen from the cave.

In other moods, people acknowledge that wealth is produced, but, following Marx, view production as exclusively a matter of using *physical* labor to transform natural resources into finished products. In the midst of the "computer revolution," when technological discoveries are shrinking yesterday's multi-million-dollar room-sized computer down to the size of a briefcase and making it available for the cost of a used car, people cling to the notion that the mind is irrelevant to production.

On the premise that muscles are the source of wealth, the accumulation of wealth by corporations is a sign of the exploitation of the workers: the economic power of those who do not sweat and toil can have been gained only by preying upon those who do.

In a final variant, people do not deny entirely the role of intelligence in production, but view wealth as an anonymous social product unrelated to individual choice, effort, ambition and ability. If today's standard of living is due equally to the work of Thomas Edison, any random factory worker, and the corner panhandler, then everyone has a right to an equal "share of the pie." Again, the conclusion is that any man's possession of above-average wealth means that he has exercised some magical power of diverting the "fair share" of others into his own pocket.

In any variant, the immortal refutation of "the goods are here" approach to wealth is provided by *Atlas Shrugged*. As Galt says in explaining the meaning of the strike he leads, "We've heard it shouted that the industrialist is a parasite, that his workers support him, create his wealth, make his luxury possible— and what would happen to him if they walked out? Very well. I propose to show to the world who depends on whom, who supports whom, who is the source of wealth, who makes whose livelihood possible and what happens to whom when who walks out."

Once it is admitted that wealth is the product of individual thought and effort, the question arises: who should own that product? On an ethics of rational egoism, the answer is: he who created it. On the moral premise of altruism, however, the answer is: anyone who needs it. Altruism specializes in the separation of creator and his creation, of agent and beneficiary, of action and consequences.

According to altruism, if you create a good and I do not, that very fact deprives you of the right to that good and makes me its rightful owner, on the principle, "from each according to his ability; to each according to his need."

On that premise, anyone who possesses a good needed by another must surrender it or be guilty of theft. Thus altruism turns businessmen into extortionists, since they charge money for relinquishing possession of the goods rightfully belonging to others. A government whose political power is directed to protecting business's control over their product is, from the altruist standpoint, initiating physical force against the rightful owners of those goods. By this moral code, the economic power of business *is* political power, since the wealth of businesses is protected by government, instead of being turned over to the needy.

Altruism engenders an inverted, death-dealing version of property rights: ownership by right of non-production.

Is this an exaggeration? Look at the statements of those who take altruism seriously—for example, George Will, who lauds the "willingness to sacrifice private desires for public ends."

Urging "conservatives" to embrace the welfare state, Will quotes approvingly from the 1877 Supreme Court case of *Munn v. Illinois,* in which the court ruled that a State could regulate the prices of private businesses: "When, therefore, one devotes his property to a use in which the public has an interest, he, in effect, grants to the public an interest in that use, and must submit to be controlled by the public for the common good, to the extent of the interest *he has thus created.*" (emphasis added)

One must submit to be controlled—why? Because he created a value. Controlled—by whom? By "the public"—i.e., by all those who have not created that value.

Philosophically, the equivocation between economic power and political power rests on the metaphysics of causeless wealth and the ethics of parasitism. Psychologically, it appeals to a fear of self-reliance, the fear that is the dominant emotion of the kind of dependent mentality Ayn Rand called the "second-hander."

The second-hander feels that the distinction between the dollar and the gun is "purely theoretical." He has long ago granted the smiles and frowns of others the power to dictate his values and control his behavior. Feeling himself to be metaphysically incompetent and society to be omnipotent, he believes that having to rely on himself would mean putting his life in jeopardy. A society of freedom, he feels, is a society in which he could be deprived of the support on which his life depends.

When you talk to him in your terms, telling him that we are all separate, independent equals who can deal with each other either by reason or by force, he literally doesn't know what you are talking about. Having abandoned his critical faculty, any idea, any offer, any deal is compulsory to him if it is accompanied by social pressure. You may tell him that in order to survive, man must be free to think. But he lacks the concepts of independent survival, independent thought, and even of objective reality; his credo is Erich Fromm's: "Love is the only sane and satisfactory answer to the problem of human existence." (*Man for Himself,* p. 133)

I will conclude with another scenario. Imagine that you survive a shipwreck and have to steer your lifeboat to one of two desert islands where you will have to remain for several years. On each island there is one inhabitant. The western island is the property of a retired multi-millionaire, who lives there in high luxury, with a mansion, two swimming pools and all the accoutrements of great wealth. The eastern island is inhabited by a propertyless beachcomber who lives in rags and eats whatever fruit and fish he can scrounge up. Let's add that the millionaire is an egoist and strict capitalist, while the beachcomber is a saint of altruism who will gladly share his mud hut with you. Would you, or anyone, head east to escape being "exploited" by the millionaire's economic power?

So much for the idea that one is threatened by the economic power of others.

But one doesn't have to resort to desert-island fables. The same practical demonstration of the life-giving nature of economic power and the fatal nature of unbounded political power is provided by the hundreds of thousands of people—Boat People they are called—who cling to their pathetic, overloaded vessels, fleeing the lands of the gun and heading toward whatever islands of even semi-capitalism they can find left in the world.

If for every hundred refugees seeking to flee collectivist dictatorships we could exchange one intellectual who urges us to fear the dollar and revere the gun, America might once again become a land of liberty and justice for all.

The Philosophical Origins of Antitrust

John B. Ridpath

This article was first published in The Objectivist Forum *in 1980.*

The Philosophical Origins of Antitrust

John B. Ridpath

The antitrust laws of the United States are an obscene violation of individual rights that have thrown American business into a no-man's land of non-objective law. As Ayn Rand states,

> The antitrust laws give the government the power to prosecute and convict any business concern in the country any time it chooses. The threat of sudden destruction, of unpredictable retaliation for unnamed offenses, is a much more potent means of enslavement than explicit dictatorial laws.[1]

Antitrust is a political cancer, clearly alien to the founding principles of this country. Where did it come from?

Unlike most statist measures adopted in this country, antitrust laws were not a European import. They were originated and fostered by Americans—predominantly, by American *conservatives*. In particular, the conceptual underpinnings of American antitrust were supplied by a prominent conservative economist, the founder of the "Chicago School" of economics: Frank H.

Knight. It was Frank Knight's theoretical work on competition that, more than any other single factor, gave American antitrust its unparalleled virulence.

The role of Frank Knight's metaphysical and epistemological ideas in the development of his theory of competition amounts to a textbook case in the political impact of basic philosophical premises.

Antitrust was born in the late nineteenth century, with the passage of the Interstate Commerce Act (1887) and the Sherman Act (1890). The movement began as a reaction to the distortions caused by previous government interventions in the market—especially government favors granted to the railroad industry.[2]

In its early years, antitrust had neither an intellectual base nor any justification in economic theory. In fact, most economists of the time favored trusts and other forms of large-scale business combinations. The only intellectual content in the early antitrust campaign derived from a naked equivocation between political power and economic power, as in Senator Sherman's pronouncement: "If we will not endure a king as a political power, we should not endure a king over the production, transportation and sale of any of the necessaries of life."[3]

Lacking a theoretical base, the early antitrust crusade proceeded somewhat meekly, in an *ad hoc* manner. At this stage, antitrust merely attempted to prescribe limits—however vague—beyond which businesses must not go. Wrong as early antitrust was, it at least did not impose any standard of "proper" business behavior, and businessmen were presumed innocent of the "crime" of "restraining trade," until specific charges of wrongdoing were raised.

But the legal environment for businessmen was to change dramatically in the twentieth century, as antitrust began to embody an (allegedly) pro-competition policy. Now businesses were faced with the task of proving that they were sufficiently competitive. The ominous significance of this re-orientation is explained by A. D. Neale:

> with a positive aim, even minor [alleged] impairments of competition will tend to be compared with some ideal model that it is hoped to achieve and will look worse in comparison. . . . Economic theory is believed to have established a presumption that any impairment of competition is harmful, and those concerned with enforcing antitrust have come to take this presumption as their rule of thumb.[4]

This "ideal model" that "economic theory" supplied to antitrust is the doctrine of "perfect competition"—the doctrine formalized by Frank Knight. Knight's theory of perfect competition provided antitrust with the theoretical teeth that have made American antitrust unique in its scope and severity. It is Knight's doctrine that has come to serve as the theoretical basis for harassment of businesses, expropriation of property, penalization of success and imprisonment of businessmen.

What is Knight's doctrine?

The perfect competition model in its full form first appeared in Knight's highly influential work, *Risk, Uncertainty and Profit*, first published in 1921. That work grew out of Knight's interest in the effect of competition upon profit. Knight held that part of a firm's profits—a part he termed "pure profit"—had no actual economic function. This "pure" profit, he wrote, "is *not* properly a 'reward for risk-taking,' . . . [and it] is not the price of the service of its recipient, but a 'residual,' the one true residual."[5]

In this evaluation of "pure" profits, Knight assumed a collectivist standard: "pure" profits, he held, make no contribution to the "general welfare," and this is what marks them as economically superfluous.

Knight went on to ask himself what market conditions would be required to eliminate all "pure" profit, and leave business with only those earnings that are useful to society. Knight constructed in his mind a fantasy world in which all those profit-eliminating conditions obtained. This "ideal" world is the perfect competition model.

The world of perfect competition is described by Knight as having the following characteristics. Everyone is omniscient concerning all economic opportunities, all factors of production are infinitely mobile and infinitely divisible, every market contains an infinite number of buyers and sellers, no one has any "sentimental" (i.e., nonpecuniary) interest in anyone else, all the products of competing firms are identical and no innovation occurs in any field.

Under these conditions, Knight held, no business would be able to earn more than would be required to cover its operating costs plus an interest return on its capital investment. No part of "society's income" would be withdrawn as "pure" profit.

The most glaringly obvious feature of the world depicted in the perfect competition model is its unreality. As George Reisman has thoroughly demonstrated in his article "Platonic Competition,"[6] the entire theory is neither drawn from nor applicable to reality.

The basic fact of reality is that everything that exists has an identity—everything, including human knowledge, is specific and finite. A world of undifferentiated products, traded by infinitely numerous and infinitely knowledgeable beings is metaphysically impossible. Knight's "ideal" world is one containing entities without identity and men without personal interests and individual judgment—i.e., without selves. Yet, as Dr. Reisman writes,

> This "concept" divorced from reality, this Platonic "ideal of perfection" drawn from non-existence to serve as the "standard" for judging existence . . . . is at the base of antitrust prosecutions, which have forced businessmen to operate under conditions approaching a reign of terror.[7]

Had he been confronted with the charge that his theory was

totally unrealistic, Knight would have replied, "Exactly. How could it be otherwise?" Knight openly acknowledged that the perfect competition model does not correspond to reality: "such a system is inherently self-defeating and could not exist in the real world."[8]

In general, Knight held that all economic theory is unavoidably severed from the real world: "All 'economic' theory in the proper sense of the word, is purely abstract and formal, without content."[9]

The theory of perfect competition is the product of Knight's basic philosophy, his views concerning reality, causality, concepts and theory. Knight was no amateur dabbler in philosophy. In graduate school, he first majored, and then minored, in philosophy, and he kept up an active involvement with philosophy throughout his career. He was thoroughly aware of and serious about the philosophical foundations of his work. Knight was quite eclectic philosophically; he showed no complete allegiance to any one school. Overall, however, his outlook is Platonic (this imperfect world is largely closed to reason), with a Kantian twist (reason can create its own world).

In metaphysics, Knight held throughout his life to a single conviction: that reality is permeated by causeless, unpredictable change. The disruptive influence of chance, accidental occurrences swamps whatever tendency toward order and constancy the world might contain. In the preface to the 1957 reprint of *Risk, Uncertainty and Profit*, Knight wrote:

> It is still my conviction that contingency or "chance" is an unanalyzable fact of nature. . . . Chance is more than human ignorance of causality which is "really" absolute; that idea was always a dogma, an intellectual prejudice.[10]

On the surface, reality seems to be made up of things—entities—each having its own identity, each subject to the law of causality and behaving in orderly, predictable ways. But, Knight believed, this is merely a convenient illusion.

> We have, then, our dogma which is the presupposition of knowledge, in this form; that the world is made up of *things*, which, *under the same circumstances*, always behave *in the same way*.[11]

For Knight, the world is not a place, but a *process*, a process of continual novelty and transformation in which there is no constancy, no causality, no laws of nature, no enduring facts and no absolutes other than flux and ignorance. We live in a world where nothing is quite what it is, where everything is either just about to be something, or has just been something, and is now changing from what it wasn't quite, to what it won't quite be.

In taking this view of the world, Knight joined a very old and very wrong tradition in Western philosophy, a tradition founded by the pre-Socratic philosopher Heraclitus. Heraclitus capsulized this metaphysics in the now-famous phrase, "You can't step into the same river twice," a phrase which has created a fetid intellectual current that thinkers have been wading in ever since. Knight was led to plunge into these muddied waters by his study of Henri Bergson, a prominent nineteenth-century Heraclitean.

What of man's nature? Just as lawlessness dominates in physical reality, so irrationality is the major feature of man's nature, according to Knight. Man is dominated by momentary whims; he is unaware of his true motives (chiefly the quest for status and prestige). Man's actions—even in the area of business—are generally not purposeful, but "impulsive and capricious."[12]

But, Knight says, economics cannot deal with the irrational side of man's nature. Economics "assumes that men's acts are ruled by conscious motives,"[13] rather than by unconscious urges. In economics, "Analysis must use the concept of complete rationality—the economic man."[14] This unavoidable divergence between the assumptions of economic science and the facts of man's economic behavior

> raises the fundamental question of how far human behavior
> is inherentlysubject to scientific treatment. In his views on
> this point the author is very much of an irrationalist. In this
> view the whole interpretation of life as activity directed to-
> ward securing anything considered as really wanted, is highly
> artificial and unreal.[15]

If reality is dominated by Heraclitean contingency, and man's
nature is dominated by unconscious motives beyond scientific
treatment, what is a theoretician to do? Consistently enough,
Knight states that, in the final analysis, theoretical knowledge is
impossible. If we understand what such knowledge involves,
Knight says, we will see that the human intellect by its very nature is precluded from knowing a world in flux.

> There is, however, much question as to how far the world is
> intelligible at all …. In so far as there is "real change" in the
> Bergsonian (i.e., Heraclitean) sense it seems clear that rea-
> soning is impossible.[16]

Within the context of the dominant philosophies of his time,
Knight was not taking a unique or surprising view. He was simply conforming to then-current philosophical trends. Knight had
absorbed the basic dichotomy underlying all modern philosophy:
the Kantian false dichotomy between reality as it really is, and
reality as it appears to us from within the prison of our own minds.
For Kant, we are locked inside mental "categories" that are part
of our nature and beyond our control, while for Knight, following the neo-Kantians, we, ourselves, arbitrarily fashion our own
categories or constructs.

(Like all Kantians, Bergson and Knight did offer a non-ra-
tional source of knowledge: a mystical "intuition" which allows
the mind to enter into things and grasp them "from the inside."[17]
Knight went so far as to announce, "if our feelings tell us nothing
about reality, then we know and can know nothing about it."[18])

In his less skeptical moments, Knight allowed a limited role for scientific theory. But it is scientific theory conceived along Kantian lines. Because of the intellect's nature, Knight states, it can deal only with fixed entities, with things which are what they are, and which, accordingly, always behave in a lawful, predictable, noncontradictory way. Bergson had written, "The intellect is never quite at ease, never entirely at home, except when it is working on inert matter." Knight expressed the same idea:

> For if it is the intrinsic nature of a thing to grow and change, it cannot serve as a scientific datum. A science must have a "static" subject-matter; it must talk about things which will "stay put"; otherwise its statements will not remain true after they are made and there will be no point in making them.[20]

This leads to Knight's view of what the intellect can do, and what the nature of theory, including the theory of perfect competition, is. The intellect can create *in the mind* the static, stable world it needs as its subject matter. This static construct can then be used as a rough approximation in dealing with the dynamic and unstable real world. Using highly Platonic language, Knight states that the intellect creates an "abstract," "clean," "idealistic" world in the mind, one that is free of "the complex and often unlovely flesh and viscera of reality."[21]

There are at work in the world, according to Knight, certain stable, knowable *tendencies* (e.g., the tendency for competition to eliminate "pure" profit). These tendencies can never manifest themselves in their pure form, because of the overwhelming disruptions caused by the Heraclitean flux. Nevertheless, we can construct in our minds an artificial, lawful world in which these tendencies operate unopposed.

The resulting model, it must be stressed, does not represent an abstraction of essentials from details; it represents a flight into the fantasy world of "what if?" (e.g., "what if every buyer and seller were omniscient?"). Heraclitean contingency and human irrationality are the essentials, according to Knight's philosophy, and these are precisely what "idealizations" such as the perfect competition model must omit.

Thus, for Knight, the perfection involved here is epistemological: when the "unlovely" characteristics of reality are mentally eliminated, the product satisfies perfectly the needs of our mind. Unfortunately, it does so at the price of falsifying reality. Because of the incompatibility between the nature of the world (as flux) and the requirements of the mind (for stability), the best we can do intellectually is to use artificial constructs. In true Kantian fashion, Knight's epistemology proceeds from the assumption that the cognitive requirements of the intellect set it at odds with reality. We must choose between reason and reality. (For details on, and a refutation of, this Kantian premise, see Ayn Rand, *Introduction to Objectivist Epistemology*, Ch. VIII.)

Knight's perfect competition model was never intended to correspond to reality. It was derived from reality only in the sense that Knight took an alleged tendency from the real world and projected how it would operate in an impossible, unreal world.

In the world of perfect competition, the "pure" profits earned by entrepreneurs would not exist. Knight concluded that these profits must have their source in Heraclitean contingency. Profits, which in fact are the earned reward for intelligently and courageously producing material values, are to Knight nothing more than manna randomly sprinkled by the unknowable flux and human irrationality. This view of the source of profits laid the groundwork, which others later built upon, for taking the existence of high profits as *prima facie* evidence of uncompetitive behavior in violation of antitrust law.

The perfect competition model furnished a powerful weapon for those who possessed the statist fervor Knight lacked. Knight's pleas to remember that his model was only a theoretical ideal (!) were increasingly ignored. People naturally reasoned: if this is the ideal, then we should try to approach it in practice. Interpreting "perfect competition" in normative terms is virtually unavoidable, psychoepistemologically. Anyone who automatizes such a term will be led to employ it normatively, even if the term's originator advises against doing so. Even though, for Knight, the "perfection" involved was epistemological, for those who followed him the perfect competition model functioned as a moral and political ideal.

Even those intellectuals who did not share Knight's bizarre Bergsonian premises were attracted to his perfect competition model because of two other Kantian (or neo-Kantian) doctrines: altruism and pragmatism.

Pragmatism has been the dominant philosophical school among American intellectuals in the twentieth century. Pragmatism's scorn of absolutes and of principles (which Knight shared) leads its adherents to take a range-of-the-moment view of the world. Such a view, when applied to economics—a science where the central focus is on long-range consequences—produces disastrous results (the most notable being Keynesianism). A pragmatist approach in economics centers one's attention on the distribution or "allocation" of goods, rather than on their source in production. As Ayn Rand put it in *Atlas Shrugged:*

> The problem of production, they tell you, has been solved and deserves no study or concern; the only problem left for your "reflexes" to solve is now the problem of distribution. Who solved the problem of production? Humanity, they answer. What was the solution? The goods are here. How did they get here? Somehow. What caused it? Nothing has causes.[22]

The implicit premise of the perfect competition theory is that businessmen are to be conceived not as productive creators but as cogs facelessly involved in a process that spews out undifferentiated goods to impassive throngs—that businessmen can exist and function as selfless automatons with nothing to gain and no power to affect the process. It is the improper focus on distribution and consumption that made possible this notion of a "perfectly competitive" businessman.

Again, quoting from *Atlas Shrugged:*

> Frantic cowards who posture as defenders of industrialists now define the purpose of economics as "an adjustment between the unlimited desires of men and the goods supplied in limited quantity." Supplied—by whom? Blank-out.[23]

Or, in the language of a contemporary economist, Mark S. Massel:

> [Under perfect competition] resources . . . are so allocated that the largest number of consumer wants which can be met are satisfied.[24]

The altruist ideal of unrecorded service to others motivated the acceptance of the perfect competition model and its use as a standard for antitrust. The root reason why lawyers, economists, politicians and businessmen accepted this model and hold it as a virtually unchallengeable standard, is that the conduct it depicts *is* perfect according to the altruist morality. The model appeals to altruists because it describes a world in which everyone is acting to best serve the interest of the consuming public—a world in which goods are automatically distributed in such a manner that no one receives any selfish gain "at the expense of" others, and in which everyone participates in a process that gives the most satisfaction equally to all. In Knight's own words:

> Under perfect competition he [the entrepreneur] would of course be completely helpless, a mere automatic registrar of the choices of consumers.[25]

This is the moral meaning of the standard used by modern antitrust. Businessmen are being persecuted for not being sufficiently identityless, passive, altruistic servants of consumers.

Anti-reason, anti-identity, anti-causality, and anti-self—these philosophical poisons have all combined to provide the foundations for modern antitrust's assault on the most productive system man has ever known—capitalism, and on the most productive individuals in human history—the industrialists. This is not surprising. No activity, no individual, no society in *this* world will ever be deemed good or just when judged by standards drawn from non-existence.

Any theory, such as perfect competition, which is removed from and disdainful of reality will lead to the immolation of those most capable of dealing with reality. That is both the theory's effect and its ultimate purpose.

References

1   "Antitrust: The Rule of Unreason," *The Objectivist Newsletter,*
February 1962, p. 8.
2   See Alan Greenspan, "Antitrust," in *Capitalism: The Unknown Ideal.*
3   Quoted in A. D. Neale, *The Antitrust Laws of the U.S.A.* (Cambridge
University Press, 1966), p. 25.
4   Ibid., p. 29.
5   *Risk, Uncertainty and Profit* (Augustus Kelley, 1964), p. lix.
6   *The Objectivist*, August-September 1968.
7   *The Objectivist*, September 1968, p. 11.
8   *Risk, Uncertainty and Profit*, p. 193.
9   Ibid., p. xii.
10   Ibid., p. lx.
11   Ibid., p. 204.
12   Ibid., p. 52.
13   Ibid.
14   *Intelligence and Democratic Action* (Harvard University Press, 1960),
p. 72.
15   *Risk, Uncertainty and Profit*, pp. 52–3.
16   Ibid., p. 209.
17   *The Ethics of Competition* (Allen & Unwin, 1935), p. 108.
18   Ibid., p. 39.
19   *Creative Evolution* (Holt, 1911), p. 154.
20   *The Ethics of Competition*, p. 21.
21   *The Economic Organization* (Harper & Row, 1965), p. 35.
22   *Atlas Shrugged* (Signet, 1957), p. 968.
23   Ibid.
24   *Competition and Monopoly* (Doubleday, 1964), pp. 196–7.
25   *History and Method of Economics* (University of Chicago Press,
1956), p. 92.

Antitrust "Returns" With a Vengeance

Richard M. Salsman

This article was first published in The Intellectual Activist *in 1995.*

Antitrust "Returns" With a Vengeance

Richard M. Salsman

First enacted more than a century ago, the antitrust laws have been used to dismember some of America's finest companies, even to jail some of its most productive businessmen. Ayn Rand has identified these laws as "the judicial version of the doctrine of Original Sin, which presumes men to be guilty with little or no chance to be proved innocent."[1] Guilty of what? Allegedly, the businessman monopolizes production, restricts competition or harms consumers. But the disciples of antitrust believe his real "sin" is that he is supremely successful at being selfish. He must "give something back to the community," yet shows no regard for the "public interest." Altruism and populism—the same forces behind America's recent move to the right—have served to buttress the antitrust laws, both philosophically and historically.

Critics of the right often portray Ronald Reagan as having emasculated the antitrust laws. They point to the 1982 withdrawal of the thirteen-year antitrust case against IBM, to the latitude granted "vertical" mergers (those between a company and its suppliers or distributors), and to the dismissal of most complaints about "barriers to entry" under the Reagan Administration.

In fact, the Reagan Justice Department made only procedural changes in antitrust enforcement in some narrow areas, changes binding neither on judges nor on succeeding presidents. The Reagan administration strictly enforced laws against "price fixing," "predatory pricing," "intent to monopolize," and "horizontal mergers" (those between companies in the same industry). As before Reagan and even today, antitrust investigations averaged *two hundred a year* in the mid-1980s. Imprisonment for antitrust violations also continued: in 1985 more than a dozen executives from electrical contracting firms were jailed.[2]

The Reagan administration dropped the case against IBM primarily because during thirteen years of litigation the company had lost its large market share in computers. Still, IBM was forced to sell a major subsidiary, at a price far below its worth, to Control Data—the competitor that had brought the initial suit. Two years later, AT&T was broken up owing to its "dominant" position and to complaints from competitor MCI. The Reagan administration argued that antitrust law must apply to ensure "competition" in newly deregulated industries. Industries deregulated under President Carter became subject to antitrust under President Reagan. Thus, either companies are granted monopolies, subjected to regulation, and given antitrust exemptions (such as utilities, the post office and Amtrak) or they are "deregulated" and subjected to the injustices of antitrust law. Only the form of regulation is changed. Either way, freedom is not allowed.

Ever since the departure of Reagan's early antitrust appointees, the statists have agitated for a "return" to antitrust—with a vengeance. The Bush and Clinton administrations have granted them their wish.[3] Consider the antitrust attacks on American and other airlines, on pharmaceutical companies such as Pfizer, on

Wal-Mart, and on Microsoft. Each has joined the long list of business success stories in America—and thereby has also joined the antitrust hit list.

The U.S. airline industry was substantially deregulated in the late 1970s, after years of strict government control. Since then, the output of this industry expanded enormously, whether measured by new airlines formed, passenger miles flown, or cities served. Meanwhile, "price wars" proliferated and prices plummeted. What was the airlines' reward? An antitrust suit filed by the Bush administration for "price fixing." Settled in 1994, the case alleged that the major airlines "fixed prices through technologically advanced fare and reservation systems, created by American and United (and used by most travel agents). These airlines were forced to issue refunds and to share their reservation systems with competitors, or else divest them.

U.S. pharmaceutical companies, considered the best in the world, came under attack by the Clinton administration during its push for socialized medicine in 1993. An industry that has shown remarkably creative powers and the ability to mass-produce affordable drugs nevertheless was threatened with price controls and an antitrust suit for "price gouging" and "excess profits." After abandoning this attack Clinton launched another, targeting hospital mergers as "anti-competitive," even though they reduce medical costs.[4]

Not nationally known until the 1980s, Wal-Mart Stores grew into the largest U.S. retailer by selling in small markets, offering a wider selection of items at lower prices than did local merchants. The company created a revolution in "discount retailing," buying name-brand goods (especially pharmaceuticals) in bulk and selling them cheaply. Wal-Mart's profits soared and its founder, the late Sam Walton, became the country's wealthiest man. In 1993 the company was found guilty under antitrust law of "predatory pricing," i.e., of temporarily selling below cost to run rivals out of business and raise prices later.[5] Local pharmacies initiated the antitrust suit and received treble damage awards.

As in the past, today's companies are charged with being "anti-competitive" under a variety of pricing policies. The drug companies are said to be guilty of setting prices that are too high; Wal-Mart of setting prices that are too low; the airlines of setting prices that are too similar. Under antitrust, once a firm attains a certain level of importance it will be found guilty no matter what pricing policy it chooses. Its "sin" is that it has become successful and productive enough to influence prices.

The trustbusters claim to target cases in which firms restrict output and raise prices. In fact, the firms mentioned above tended to generate higher output at lower prices—and to profit handsomely doing so. So much for the alleged motive of defending the consumer.

That antitrust takes aim at a company's success and stature is obvious in the recent case against software-giant Microsoft. With MS-DOS and Windows, Microsoft provides nearly 50 percent of the operating systems governing the internal operations of microcomputers. The company also holds a respectable share of the market in word processing, database and spreadsheet programs. It produces 25 percent of all software sold worldwide. Twenty-five years ago the company did not even exist. Most computers were big "mainframes" housed within large firms. There were no personal computers.

Bill Gates, founder and head of Microsoft, helped change all that. He quit Harvard and devoted all his waking hours to writing computer software and selling it. He developed programs that took personal computers out of the domain of tinkerers and into widespread use; there are now 140 million personal computers worldwide. Started in 1974, Microsoft's sales today approach $4 billion and its profits exceed those of all competitors combined. Software output has skyrocketed and software prices have plummeted. By age forty, Bill Gates was the country's richest man, worth $9 billion.

Despite Gates's enormous productivity, *Fortune* magazine wonders whether he is "the information economy's equivalent of a robber baron."[6] And the least of Microsoft's competitors has found a friendly ear among the trustbusters. In 1990 an obscure maker of computer "mouse" devices named Z-nix, a company with $6 million in sales, sued Microsoft for monopolizing the computer software market.[7]

The Federal Trade Commission under Bush interviewed Microsoft's disgruntled competitors to build a case against the company. Many larger competitors financed the legal briefs used by the government. Some competitors complained that Microsoft impeded their software sales by announcing plans to introduce new software products. Microsoft had adopted this practice to enhance profits: potential users were allowed to pre-test software for "bugs" and invite improvements. Others' sales are "impeded" only because Microsoft's deliveries are credible and because consumers want superior products compatible with a widely accepted standard. Microsoft was also criticized, not only for its market share in operating systems, but for its ability to obtain favorable terms from its licensees.

To avoid being broken up, in 1994 Microsoft signed a "consent decree" with the Justice Department, requiring it to separate its internal departments for operating systems and application programs, *to disclose key operating system information to competitors,* and to stop releasing software early for customer pretesting. These sanctions are similar to those imposed in past cases such as Standard Oil (1911) and ALCOA (1945). Apart from being a rank injustice, they will undercut Microsoft's creativity and profitability. And even if Microsoft complies, it is not free. Consent decrees are no guarantee a company will be left alone; AT&T signed decrees in the years prior to its dismemberment and is still subject to the day-to-day rulings of a federal judge.

There is every sign that the attacks on Microsoft will escalate. Federal District judge Stanley Sporkin recently rejected the Microsoft decree as too lax, with no guarantee of restoring "competitive balance" to the market for operating systems. He argued that the decree does not satisfy "the public interest," the standard given specifically in the Tunney Act (1974) allowing judicial review of antitrust actions. In his ruling Sporkin complained that Microsoft "has a monopolistic position in a field that is central to this country's well-being, not only for the balance of this century, but also for the 21st century." If the decree were approved, "the message will be that Microsoft is so powerful that neither the market nor the Government is capable of dealing with all of its monopolistic practices." Thus, he concluded, Microsoft is "a potential threat to this nation's economic well-being."[8] The Justice Department has since tried to mollify Sporkin by hinting at potential future antitrust reprisals against Microsoft.

One perceptive account of the case that rejects the "robber baron" myth as well as antitrust laws argues that "until minds are changed, Bill Gates and other tycoons of America's information age are going to be sullied—and perhaps shackled—by the mistaken vision of antitrust."[9]

This "vision" says that the able must be sacrificed to mediocrities, that the most successful owe the most to the group, that achievement and pride are sins. The contradictions of antitrust stem from conservatives' attempt to seek the impossible: a defense of capitalism based on altruism. These alleged defenders of capitalism passed the antitrust laws and gave them a philosophical defense. That is why the laws are contradictory, why they are arbitrarily enforced, why conservative fingerprints are all over them, and why their injustice has continued unchanged in recent times.

The first antitrust law in the U.S., the Sherman Act (1890), was pushed by conservatives. Its sponsor, Republican Senator Sherman of Ohio, despaired of income inequality and concentrations of capital. He conceded that big business did lower prices, but complained that "this saving of cost goes to the pockets of the producer."[10] He warned that "the popular mind is agitated with problems that may disturb the social order," and insisted that Congress must heed popular fears "or be ready for the socialist, the communist, and the nihilist."[11] Sherman and his fellow conservatives could not defend capitalism on its proper base of rational self-interest and man's rights. They embraced populism, which holds the "popular will" as the standard of the good. Uniting altruism, majority rule, and the labor theory of value, populism says business exists to serve the "public interest" and businessmen are parasitical "robber barons."

Antitrust theory stems partly from the conservatives' unwillingness to identify capitalism's essential nature as the only social system protecting man's right to live rationally and self-ishly. Instead, conservatives define capitalism as the system of competition. Thus, they observe any lessening of competition as an open invitation to socialism. They defend socialist-style laws, such as antitrust, so as to "pre-empt" socialism.

Conservatives do worse than merely hold that "competition" is the essence of capitalism. They hold to a "pure and perfect" model of capitalist competition. According to this view, each industry should comprise numerous producers and potential entrants must have equal and costless access to it. Each producer must be devoid of any power to influence price or his negligible market share. All products and services must be indistinguishable, so there is no need for advertising. Profits are minimal, as no company or product stands out. Everyone has "perfect information" about markets. There is to be intense "competition," but if anyone is actually *seen* competing or indeed *winning* a competition that is evidence of "market failure," necessitating government intervention to "fix" the offending defect.

This theory of markets, made explicit in the 1920s, enlarged the scope of antitrust, transforming it from a weapon to be used on a single seller into one to be used on industries consisting of many sellers. Monopoly was simply redefined to mean any large market share held by an industry's leading firms. That is the standard used today. In other cases, a company is defined as a single-seller simply by narrowly defining its market. By such arbitrariness, the antitrust hit list is expanded.

There has never been a factual counterpart to the "perfect competition" theory of markets in the whole history of capitalism. Yet it forms the base of antitrust law.[12] Any market that falls short of this platonic ideal (and all must) is a threat to "competition," deserving of censure under antitrust. As John Ridpath has observed, altruism is the reason why:

> The altruist ideal of unrewarded service to others motivated the acceptance of the perfect competition model and its use as a standard of antitrust. The root reason why lawyers, economists, politicians and businessmen accepted this model and hold it as a virtually unchallengeable standard is that the conduct it depicts *is* perfect according to the altruist morality. The model appeals to altruists because it describes a world in which everyone is acting to best serve the interest of the consuming public—a world in which goods are automatically distributed in such a manner that no one receives any selfish gain "at the expense" of others, and in which everyone participates in a process that gives the most satisfaction equally to all. This is the moral meaning of the standard used by modern antitrust. Businessmen are being persecuted for not being sufficiently identity-less, passive, altruistic servants of consumers.[13]

Capitalism brings active competitions which many companies actually *win*. Altruism, in contrast, sides with the losers, with the mediocrities of the business world, and puts the force of antitrust law on their side. (More than 90 percent of all antitrust cases are filed by private litigants—by envious competitors resentful of the victors.) Altruism is the morality that inspires economists to dream up such unreal models of how a capitalist system should work, a testament to the fact that economic theories rest, ultimately, on basic philosophic premises. As M. Northrup Buechner has explained:

> For about the last one hundred years, economic thought has rested on the following logical chain: selfishness is evil; capitalism is based on selfishness; therefore capitalism is evil *and must have evil results.* The rational purpose of economics is to identify, interpret and explain the results of a free economy's operation. Altruism assured economists in advance that those results were evil. The consequence has been . . . a blizzard of bizarre theories and constructs.[14]

Not the liberals but the conservative economists—those associated with the "Chicago school" of economics—have been the ones most responsible for the "perfect competition" model and antitrust doctrine. Frank Knight, a founder of the Chicago school, and Christian philosopher, first spelled out the "ideal" of perfect competition in 1921.[15] He secured a lasting role for antitrust by grounding it philosophically—in altruism. Knight believed the ethical standard for judging competition was "social justice," based on a "Christian conception of goodness" which is "the antithesis of competitive." According to Knight, the only justification for a competitive system is that the most productive men are encouraged "to make the greatest possible addition to the total social dividend."[16] Laws must preserve those who lose in what he derisively called "the game" of business.

Friedrich Hayek, who spent nearly a decade at Chicago and shares the school's premises, defended antitrust similarly and on the claim that private property is often "an undesirable and harmful privilege." "When I speak of 'Free Enterprise' and 'Competitive Order,'" he once wrote, "the two names do not necessarily designate the same system, *and it is the system described by the second which we want.*"[17] According to Hayek, "it may be a good thing if the monopolist is treated as a sort of whipping boy of economic policy."[18]

Milton Friedman also embraces perfect competition as an ideal and writes that "the participant in a competitive market . . . is hardly visible as a separate entity." Does this describe Bill Gates? Any businessman who is "visible" is virtually a monopolist, Friedman says, and as such, "it is easy to argue that he should discharge his power . . . to further socially desirable ends."[19] Friedman knows that "widespread application of such a doctrine would destroy a free society," so he suggests that the antitrust laws should only be enforced selectively (i.e., arbitrarily, since all successful businessmen under capitalism are "visible" in some way).

Some conservative economists and legal scholars in the 1970s and 1980s criticized zealous enforcement of the antitrust laws, but did so strictly from altruist premises. The "law and economics" movement, a blend of legal positivism and Chicago school theories of competition, did not advocate the repeal of antitrust laws but noticed they were commonly enforced against innovative companies expanding output and lowering prices. This pattern was obvious. But the movement explicitly denied an objective, private property justification for business. Instead, utilitarian cost-benefit analyses were promoted to weigh the ideals of "competition" and "consumer welfare."[20] Antitrust had become a "paradox" because it was preventing business from being the true public servant it was meant to be.[21] Meanwhile, the "Public choice" school of economics, led by conservatives such as James Buchanan, complained that the selfish greed of mediocre competitors and job-promoting politicians was subverting an otherwise honorable antitrust system.[22] "Self-interest," not altruism, remained the root problem. By embracing altruism and the tribal premise that business exists to serve society, these schools could only advise procedural, not substantive, changes in antitrust.

Antitrust policy under President Reagan relied specifically on arguments from these two schools.[23] Even where enforcement was relaxed, the goal was to achieve "social efficiencies," or enhance "consumer welfare," or promote the "public interest," or deflect the "selfish" appeals of disgruntled competitors. Leniency was urged elsewhere in order to boost "U.S. competitiveness."[24] Not a single antitrust law was repealed or even amended under Reagan.

The antitrust laws are an obscene mockery of justice and are characteristic of a dictatorship. They embody non-objective law that is arbitrarily enforced. The Reagan administration challenged none of the philosophical fundamentals underlying antitrust. Enforcement was carried out by a slightly more "benevolent" dictatorship—but it was a dictatorship all the same. It ended when the liberals, recognizing that altruism's proper political counterpart is statism, returned to apply antitrust laws with a vengeance. That has been the pattern of enforcement through most of this century. The conservatives want altruism and capitalism. The liberals want altruism and statism. Either way, altruism sets the terms of policy. Antitrust has returned to the headlines, but philosophically it has never left us.

Today's conservatives, those who stand behind a "Contract with America," are primarily altruists and populists. They want to scale back the welfare state, but only because it has been shown to hurt the poor. They want tax cuts, as long as they bring in more government revenue, and then only for "working Americans," not for business or the wealthy. They are silent about the antitrust laws, about the persecution of men such as Sam Walton and Bill Gates. They may have a contract with America, but they let stand the perpetual contract that is out on the heads of American business. When capitalism's true philosophical bodyguards influence policy, the antitrust laws will be *abolished*—not simply softened or "reformed." Only then will the U.S. Justice Department dispense true justice to American business.

References

1   Ayn Rand, "Antitrust: The Rule of Unreason," *The Objectivist Newsletter,* February 1962, p. 5.

2   "Electrical Contractors Reel Under Charges That They Rigged Bids," *Wall Street Journal,* November 29, 1985. In addition to this antitrust case, of course, other successful businessmen were unjustly imprisoned under Reagan, including financier Michael Milken (under the non-objective securities laws) and hotelier Leona Helmsley (under the non-objective Federal tax code).

3   For the change under Bush see "Stronger U.S. Antitrust Action Vowed," *New York Times,* November 4, 1989; "Back to the Dark Ages of Antitrust," *Wall Street Journal,* June 17, 1992. For the change under Clinton see "A Backlog of Laissez Faire," *New York Times,* July 25, 1993; and "Reinvigorated Trustbusters on the Prowl," *Investor's Business Daily,* August 8, 1994.

4   *Economic Report of the President* (U.S. Government Printing Office, February 1995), p. 139.

5   Blant Hurt, "The Irrational Antitrust Case Against Wal-Mart," *Wall Street Journal,* October 20, 1993.

6   Brent Schendler, "What Bill Gates Really Wants," *Fortune,* January 16, 1995, p. 63.

7   James Wallace and Jim Erickson, *Hard Drive: Bill Gates and the Making of the Microsoft Empire* (Harper Collins, 1992), p. 394.

8   Cited in Edmund L. Andrews, "Judge Rejects U.S. Antitrust Pact with Microsoft," *New York Times,* February 15, 1995, and Don Clark, "Will Regulators and Rivals Hinder Microsoft," *Wall Street Journal,* February 16, 1995.

9   Tim W. Ferguson, "The Endless Application of Antitrust," *Wall Street Journal,* February 21, 1995.

10   Quoted in E. Thomas Sullivan, *The Political Economy of the Sherman Act: The First One Hundred Years* (Oxford University Press, 1991), p. 13.

11   Ibid, p. 22.

12   George Reisman, "Platonic Competition," *The Objectivist,* August-September 1968.

13   John B. Ridpath, "The Philosophical Origins of Antitrust," *The Objectivist Forum,* June 1980, p. 14.

14   M. Northrup Buechner, "Ayn Rand and Economics," *The Objectivist Forum,* August 1982, p. 6.

15   Frank H. Knight, *Risk, Uncertainty and Profit* (Houghton Mifflin Company, 1921). Knight's role is explained by Ridpath, ibid.

16   Frank H. Knight, *The Ethics of Competition* (Augustus M. Kelley, 1935), pp. 45, 48, 72.

17   Friedrich Hayek, *Individualism and Economic Order* (University of Chicago Press, 1948), pp. 114, 111 (emphasis added).

18   Friedrich Hayek, *The Constitution of Liberty* (University of Chicago Press, 1960), p. 265.

19   Milton Friedman, *Capitalism and Freedom* (University of Chicago Press,

1962), pp. 119–120.

20   Richard A. Posner, *Economic Analysis of Law* (Little, Brown, and Company, 1972).

21   Robert H. Bork, *The Antitrust Paradox* (Basic Books, 1978).

22   See Robert D. Tollison, "Public Choice and Antitrust," *The Cato Journal,* Winter 1985, pp. 905–916, who argues that this approach "will help to cast the role of antitrust in more reasonable terms" so that "a little bit more laissez-faire will be allowed to prevail."

23   *Economic Report of the President* (U.S. Government Printing Office, February 1983), pp. 101–102.

24   Malcolm Baldrige, "Rx for Export Woes: Antitrust Relief," *Wall Street Journal,* October 15, 1985. Baldrige was Secretary of Commerce under Reagan.

For Further Reading

1. *Atlas Shrugged* by Ayn Rand. The author described the theme of this novel as: "The role of the mind in man's existence— and, as corollary, the demonstration of a new moral philosophy: the morality of rational self-interest." As an adventure story and a mystery, it has been a "great read" for millions of readers since it was first published in 1957. Philosophical principles as they apply to business are demonstrated and concretized in the characters and events of the novel. Businessmen will find the novel of special interest because its heroes are great industrialists in fields such as railroads, steel, oil and copper.

2. *The Virtue of Selfishness,* by Ayn Rand, advocates an ethics of rational self-interest, based on the standard of man's life. The articles "Man's Rights" and "The Nature of Government" are included.

3. *Capitalism: The Unknown Ideal* by Ayn Rand. This collection of essays on the theory, history and current state of capitalism includes "What Is Capitalism," "The Roots of War," "The Property Status of Airwaves" and "America's Persecuted Minority: Big Business."

4. *Objectivism: The Philosophy of Ayn Rand* by Leonard Peikoff. This is the comprehensive statement of Ayn Rand's philosophy of Objectivism by its foremost living authority.

All of these books are published by Penguin USA and are available at your local bookstore. A complete listing of all of Ayn Rand's books is available at www.aynrand.org.

Information on weekly radio broadcasts of Leonard Peikoff's radio show, *Philosophy: Who Needs It,* can be found at the show's Web site http://www.pnwi.com.

Afterword: The Ayn Rand Institute

The Ayn Rand Institute (ARI) provides something unique to the best of American business: resounding moral approval.

ARI has published tens of thousands of copies of "The Meaning of Money," a speech in Ayn Rand's *Atlas Shrugged,* and distributed them to businessmen so they would have available an articulate presentation of why money is "the root of all good."

The Institute conducts annual essay contests based on Ayn Rand's *Atlas Shrugged* for graduate and undergraduate business school students. Questions for the contest focus on the moral case for capitalism and free markets. Twenty thousand dollars in cash prizes are awarded annually for this contest.

Other programs of ARI, such as placement of editorials in American newspapers and the weekly radio program, regularly take a stand in defense of the philosophical ideas necessary to build and maintain free markets and a free society.

For additional information visit ARI's Web site at www.aynrand.org.

Contributing Writers

Ayn Rand (1905–1982)
Novelist and philosopher Ayn Rand, author of *The Fountainhead, Atlas Shrugged* and many other fiction and non-fiction works, is the originator of the philosophy of Objectivism. More than 20,000,000 copies of her books have been sold.

Leonard Peikoff
Dr. Peikoff, Ayn Rand's legal and intellectual heir, is Objectivism's foremost philosopher and writer. He is the author of *Objectivism: The Philosophy of Ayn Rand,* the first systematic presentation of Ayn Rand's philosophy. He is currently a talk radio host with his own nationally broadcast weekly show, *Philosophy: Who Needs It.* Commentaries by Dr. Peikoff have appeared in such newspapers as the *Orange County Register,* the *Miami Herald,* and the *Los Angeles Times.*

Harry Binswanger
Dr. Binswanger is a professor of philosophy at the Objectivist Graduate Center, the author of *The Biological Basis for Teleological Concepts* and the editor of *The Ayn Rand Lexicon.*

Edwin A. Locke
Dr. Locke, a professor of psychology, business and management at the University of Maryland, has published more than 200 chapters and articles in professional journals, on subjects such as leadership, job satisfaction, incentives and the philosophy of science.

John B. Ridpath
Dr. Ridpath is an associate professor of economics and intellectual history at York University in Toronto, Canada.

Richard M. Salsman
Richard Salsman, is a senior vice president and senior economist at H.C. Wainwright Economics, an investment advisory firm based in Boston. He is the author of such books as *Gold and Liberty,* and his articles have appeared in the *New York Times, Investor's Business Daily,* the *Wall Street Journal, Forbes* and *Barron's.* Mr. Salsman is an adjunct fellow at the American Institute for Economic Research and is the founder of the Association of Objectivist Businessmen.

Jaana Woiceshyn
Dr. Woiceshyn teaches strategic management and business ethics at the University of Calgary, Canada.